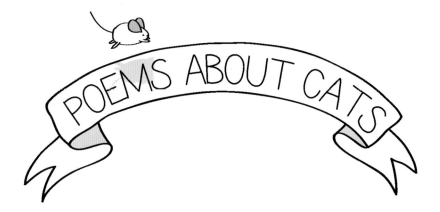

POEMS ABOUT CATS

CAT vs HUMAN

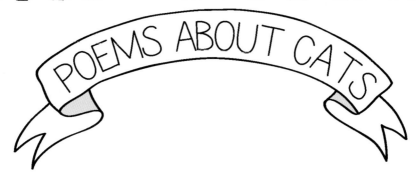

POEMS ABOUT CATS

ILLUSTRATED BY
YASMINE SUROVEC

Andrews McMeel
Publishing

Kansas City • Sydney • London

Contents

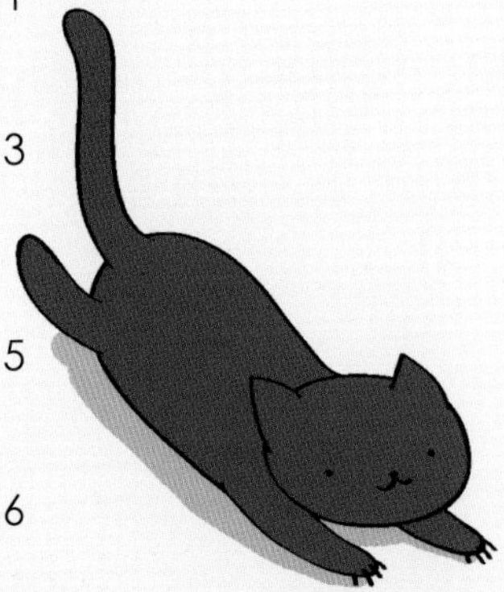

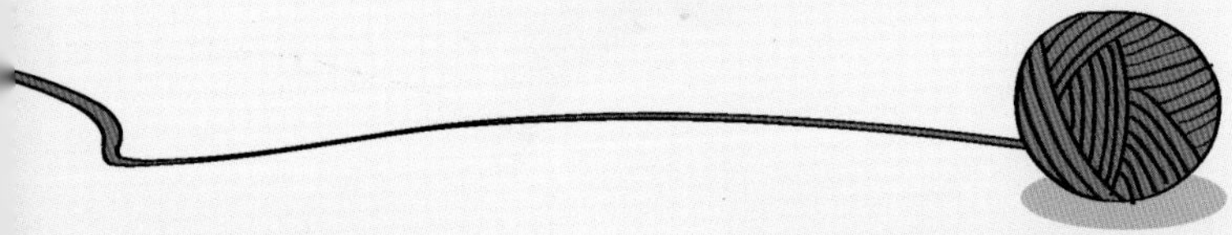

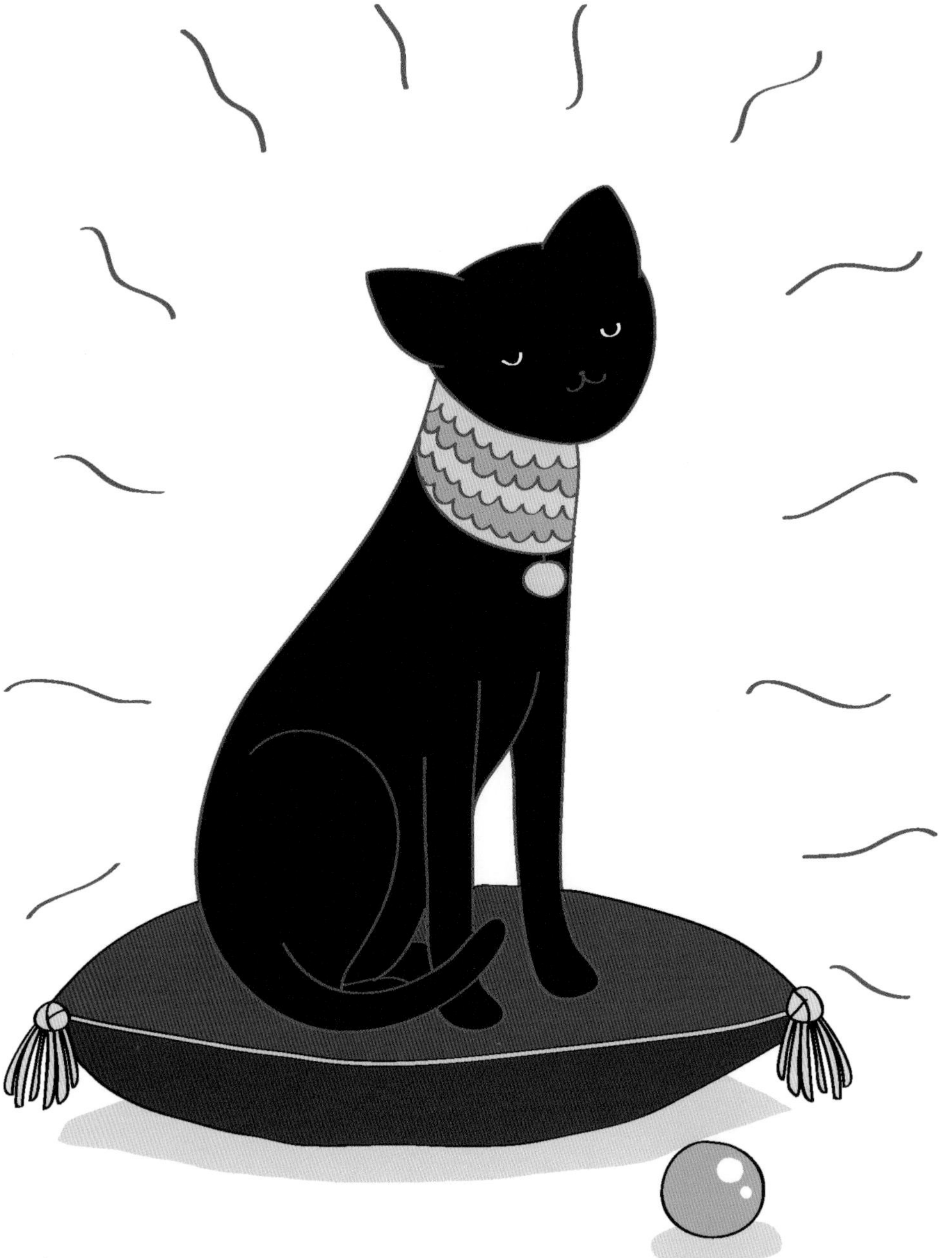

from **The Seventy-Five Praises of Ra**

found in royal tombs of Egypt

Praise be to thee, O Ra, exalted Sekhem; thou art the
Great Cat, the avenger of the gods, and the judge of words,
and the president of the sovereign chiefs, and
the governor of the holy Circle; thou art indeed the bodies
of the Great Cat.

The Tyger

William Blake

Tyger Tyger, burning bright,
In the forests of the night;
What immortal hand or eye,
Could frame thy fearful symmetry?

In what distant deeps or skies,
Burnt the fire of thine eyes?
On what wings dare he aspire?
What the hand, dare sieze the fire?

And what shoulder, & what art,
Could twist the sinews of thy heart?
And when thy heart began to beat,
What dread hand? & what dread feet?

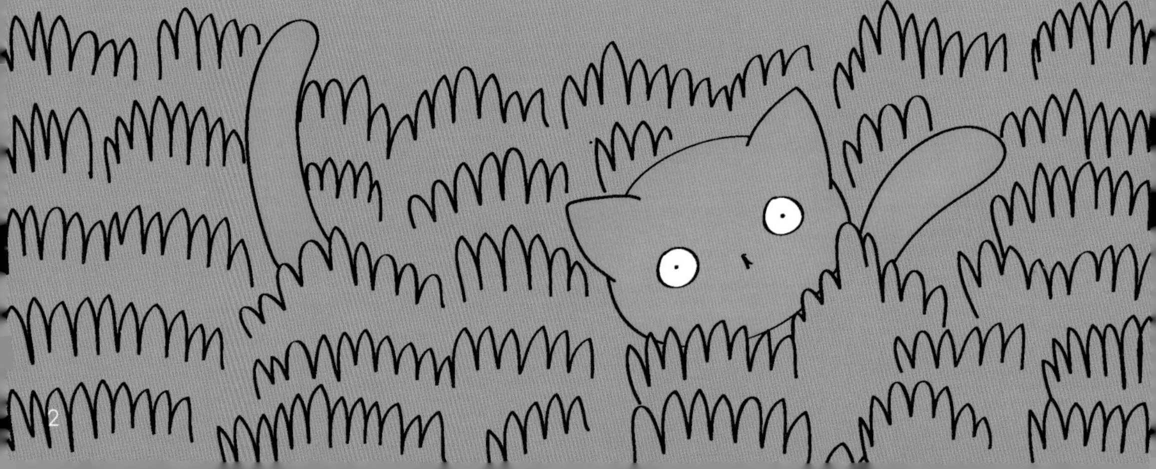

What the hammer? what the chain,
In what furnace was thy brain?
What the anvil? what dread grasp,
Dare its deadly terrors clasp?

When the stars threw down their spears
And water'd heaven with their tears:
Did he smile his work to see?
Did he who made the Lamb make thee?

Tyger Tyger burning bright,
In the forests of the night:
What immortal hand or eye,
Dare frame thy fearful symmetry?

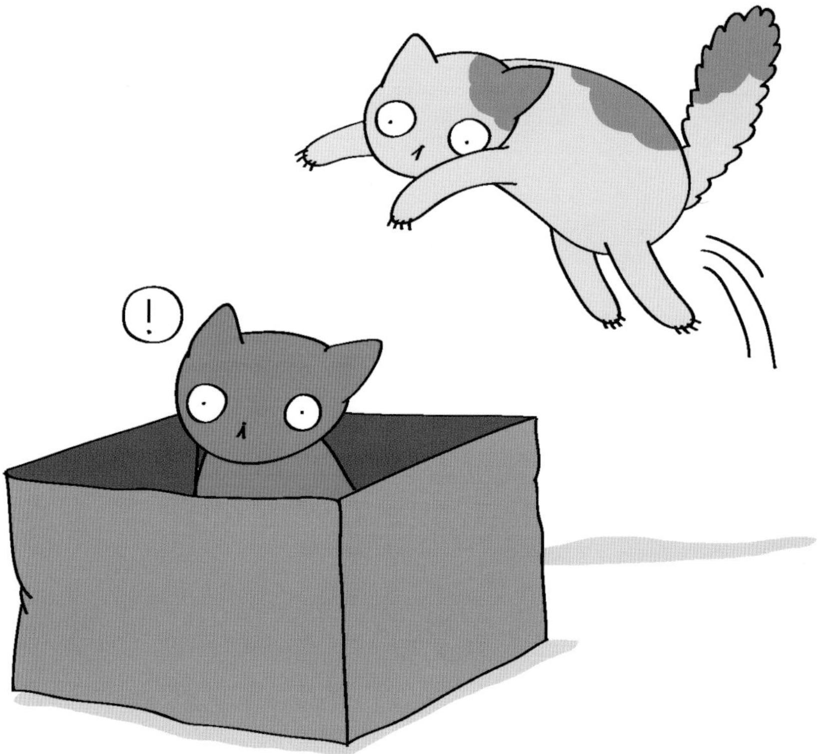
!

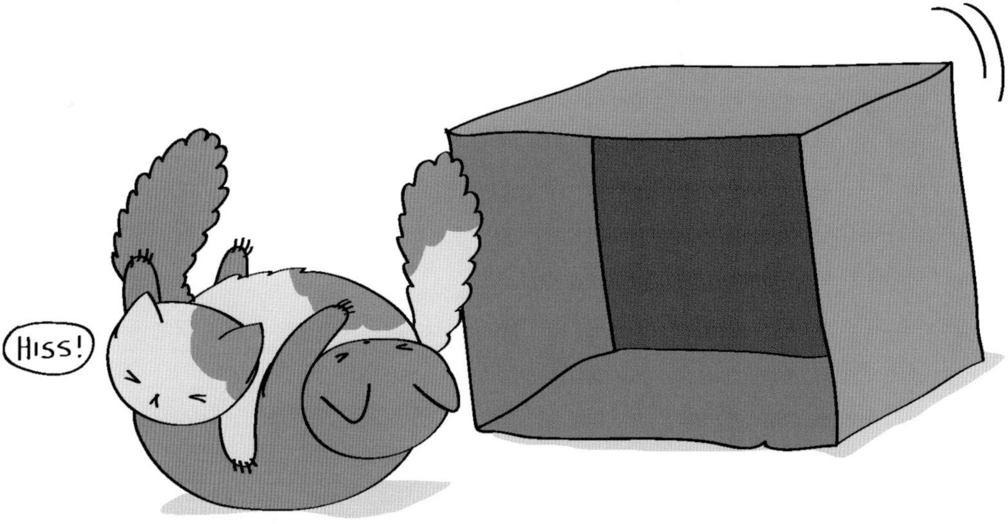
HISS!

Kilkenny Cats

There once were two cats of Kilkenny,
Each thought there was one cat too many;
So they fought and they fit,
And they scratched and they bit,
'Til (excepting their nails
And the tips of their tails),
Instead of two cats there weren't any!

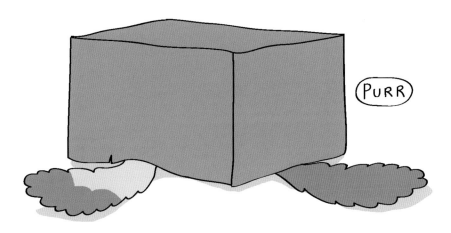

PURR

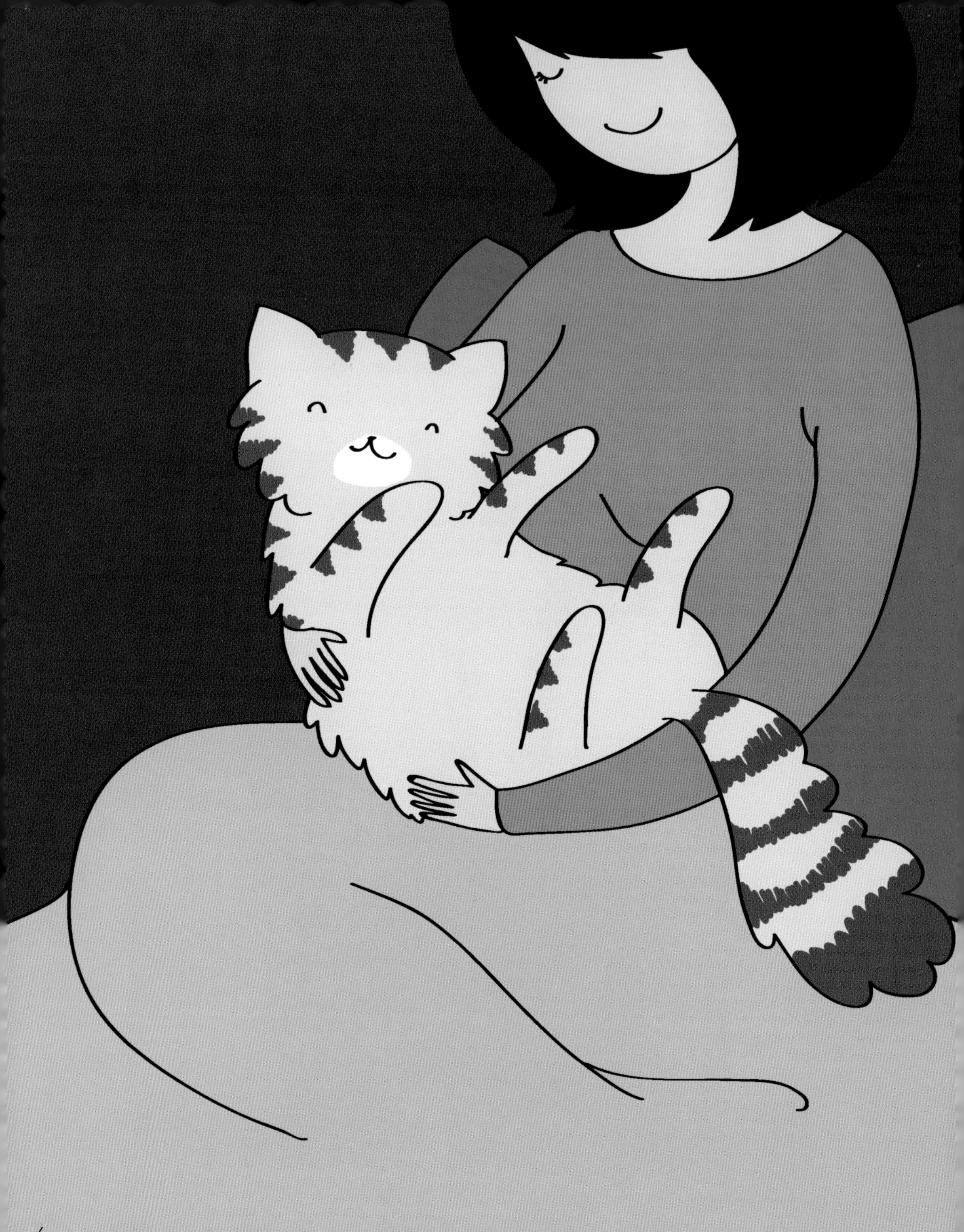

from **To a Cat**

Algernon Charles Swinburne

Stately, kindly, lordly friend,
    Condescend
Here to sit by me, and turn
Glorious eyes that smile and burn,
Gold eyes, love's lustrous meed,
On the golden page I read.

All your wondrous wealth of hair,
    Dark and fair,
Silken-shaggy, soft and bright
As the clouds and beams of night,
Pays my reverent hand's caress
Back with friendlier gentleness.

Dogs may fawn on all and some
    As they come;
You, a friend of loftier mind,
Answer friends alone in kind.
Just your foot upon my hand
Softly bids it understand.

from **Dame Wiggins of Lee, and Her Seven Wonderful Cats**

John Ruskin

Dame Wiggins of Lee
Was a worthy old soul,
As e'er threaded a nee-
dle, or wash'd in a bowl:
She held mice and rats
In such antipa-thy;
That seven fine cats
Kept Dame Wiggins of Lee.

The rats and mice scared
By this fierce whisker'd crew,
The poor seven cats
Soon had nothing to do;
So, as any one idle
She ne'er loved to see,
She sent them to school,
Did Dame Wiggins of Lee.

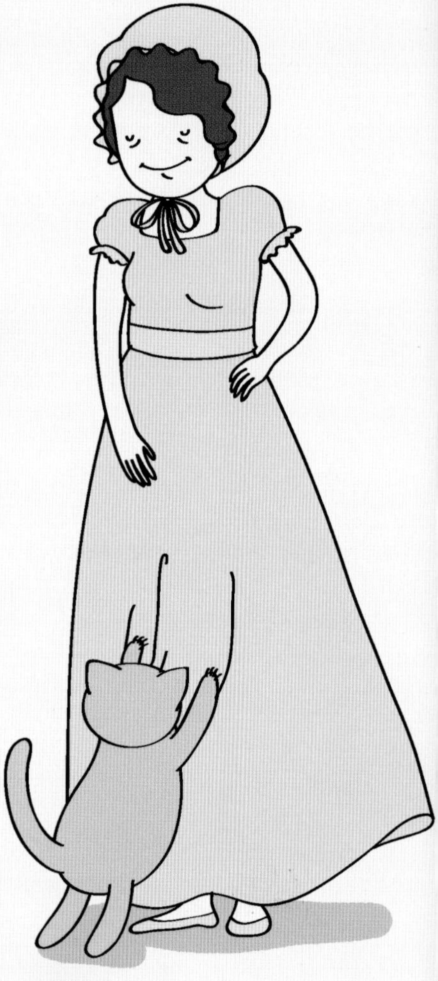

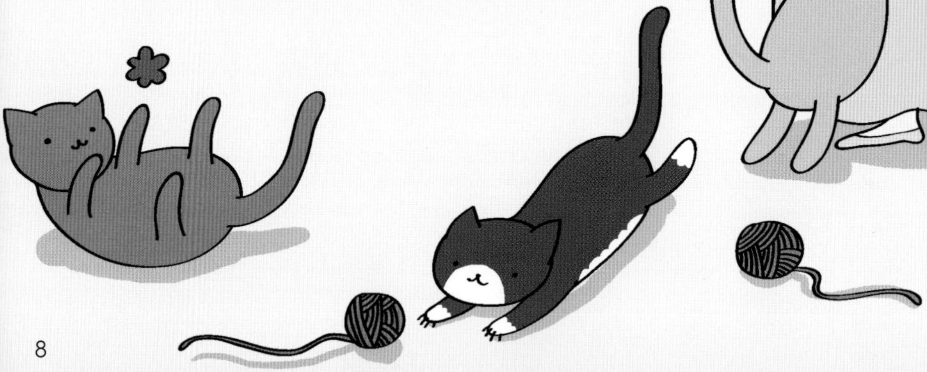

The Master soon wrote
　　That they all of them knew
How to read the word "milk"
　　And to spell the word "mew."
And they all washed their faces
　　Before they took tea:
"Were there ever such dears!"
　　Said Dame Wiggins of Lee.

He had also thought well
　　To comply with their wish
To spend all their play-time
　　In learning to fish
For stitlings; they sent her
　　A present of three,
Which, fried, were a feast
　　For Dame Wiggins of Lee.

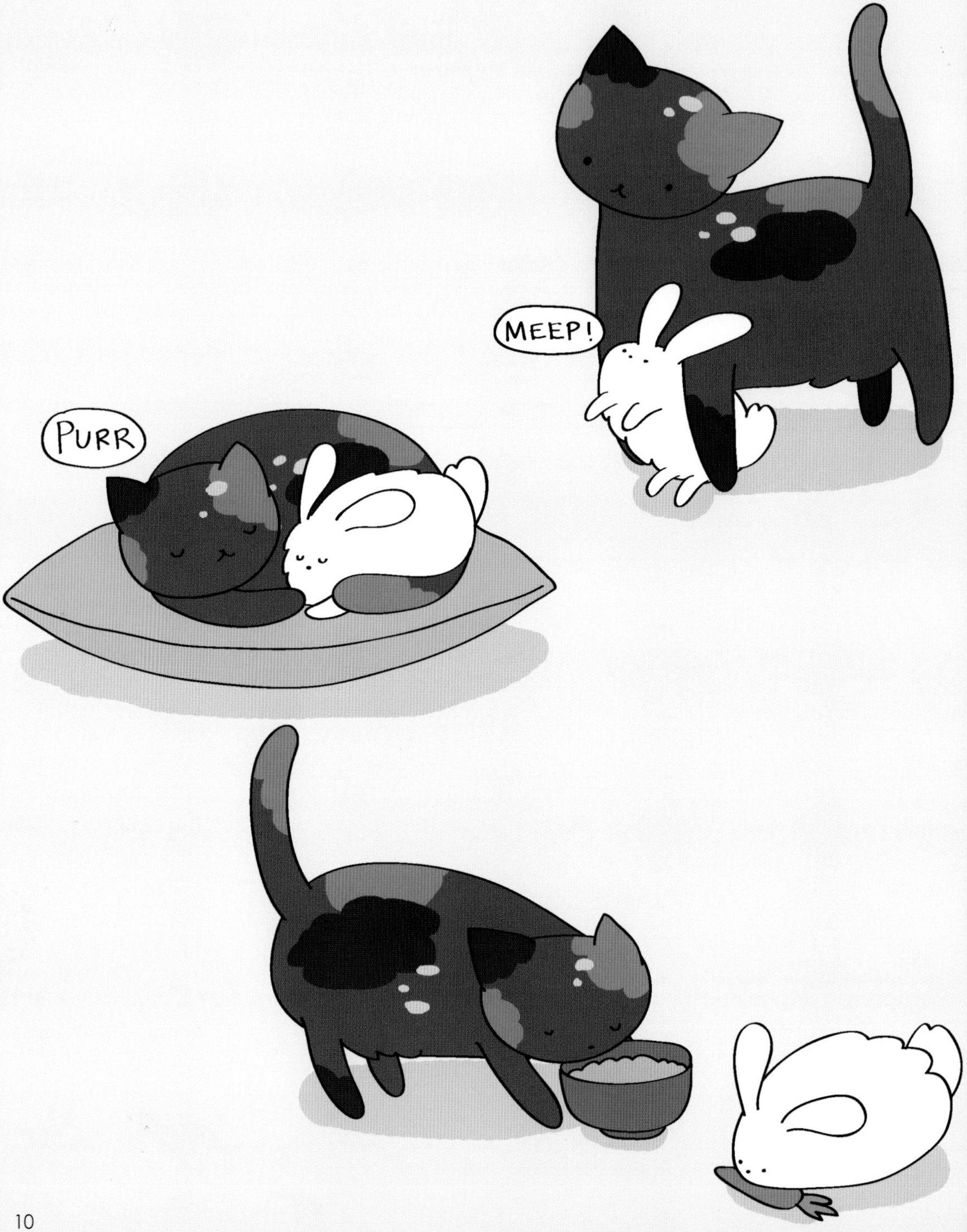
MEEP!
PURR

from **Two Songs of a Fool**

William Butler Yeats

A speckled cat and a tame hare
Eat at my hearthstone
And sleep there;
And both look up to me alone
For learning and defence
As I look up to Providence.

I start out of my sleep to think
Some day I may forget
Their food and drink;
Or, the house door left unshut,
The hare may run till it's found
The horn's sweet note and the tooth of the hound.

I bear a burden that might well try
Men that do all by rule,
And what can I
That am a wandering witted fool
But pray to God that He ease
My great responsibilities?

The Cats Have Come to Tea

Kate Greenaway

What did she see—oh, what did she see,
As she stood leaning against the tree?
Why all the Cats had come to tea.

What a fine turn out—from round about,
All the houses had let them out,
And here they were with scamper and shout.

"Mew—mew—mew!" was all they could say,
And, "We hope we find you well to-day."

Oh, what should she do—oh, what should she do?
What a lot of milk they would get through;
For here they were with "Mew—mew—mew!"

She didn't know—oh, she didn't know,
If bread and butter they'd like or no;
They might want little mice, oh! oh! oh!

Dear me—oh, dear me,
All the cats had come to tea.

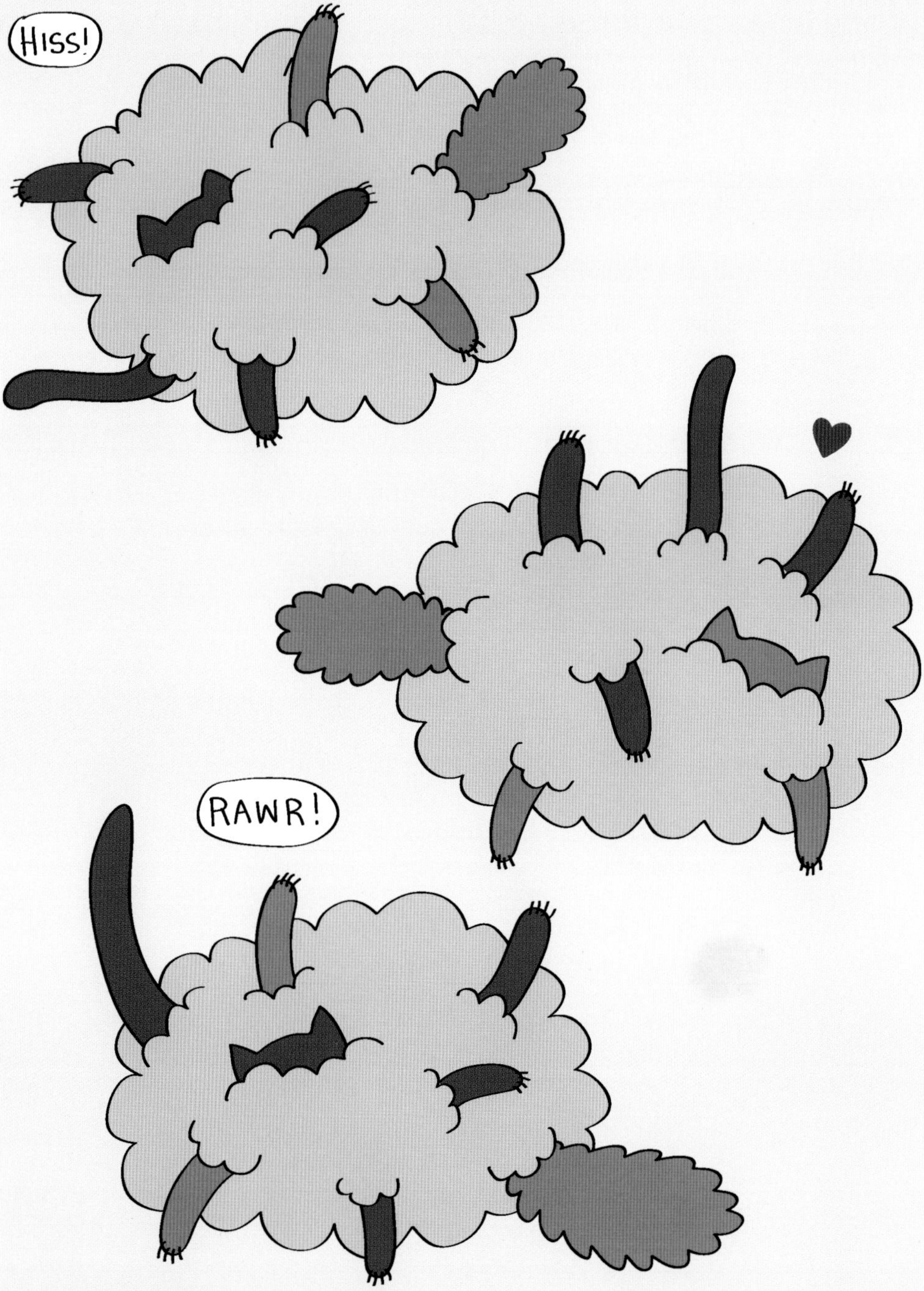
HISS!
RAWR!

An Appeal to Cats
in the Business of Love

Thomas Flatman

Ye Cats that at midnight spit love at each other,
Who best feel the pangs of a passionate Lover,
I appeal to your scratches, and your tattered furr,
If the business of love be no more than to purr.
Old Lady *Grimalkin* with her Gooseberry eyes,
Knew something when a Kitten, for why she was wise;
You find by experience the Love fit's soon o'r,
Puss! Puss! lasts not long, but turns to *Cat-whore*.

     Men ride many Miles,
     Cats tread many Tiles,
  Both hazard their necks in the Fray;
     Only Cats, when they fall
     From a House, or a Wall,
Keep their feet, mount their Tails, and away.

The Owl and the Pussy-Cat

Edward Lear

The Owl and the Pussy-cat went to sea
    In a beautiful pea-green boat,
They took some honey, and plenty of money,
    Wrapped up in a five-pound note.
The Owl looked up to the stars above,
    And sang to a small guitar,
"O lovely Pussy! O Pussy, my love,
    What a beautiful Pussy you are,
        You are,
        You are!
    What a beautiful Pussy you are!"

Pussy said to the Owl, "You elegant fowl!
    How charmingly sweet you sing!
O let us be married! too long we have tarried:
    But what shall we do for a ring?"
They sailed away, for a year and a day,
    To the land where the Bong-Tree grows,
And there in a wood a Piggy-wig stood,
    With a ring at the end of his nose,
        His nose,
        His nose,
    With a ring at the end of his nose.

"Dear Pig, are you willing to sell for one shilling
    Your ring?" Said the Piggy, "I will."
So they took it away, and were married next day
    By the Turkey who lives on the hill.
They dined on mince, and slices of quince,
    Which they ate with a runcible spoon;
And hand in hand, on the edge of the sand,
    They danced by the light of the moon,
        The moon,
        The moon,
    They danced by the light of the moon.

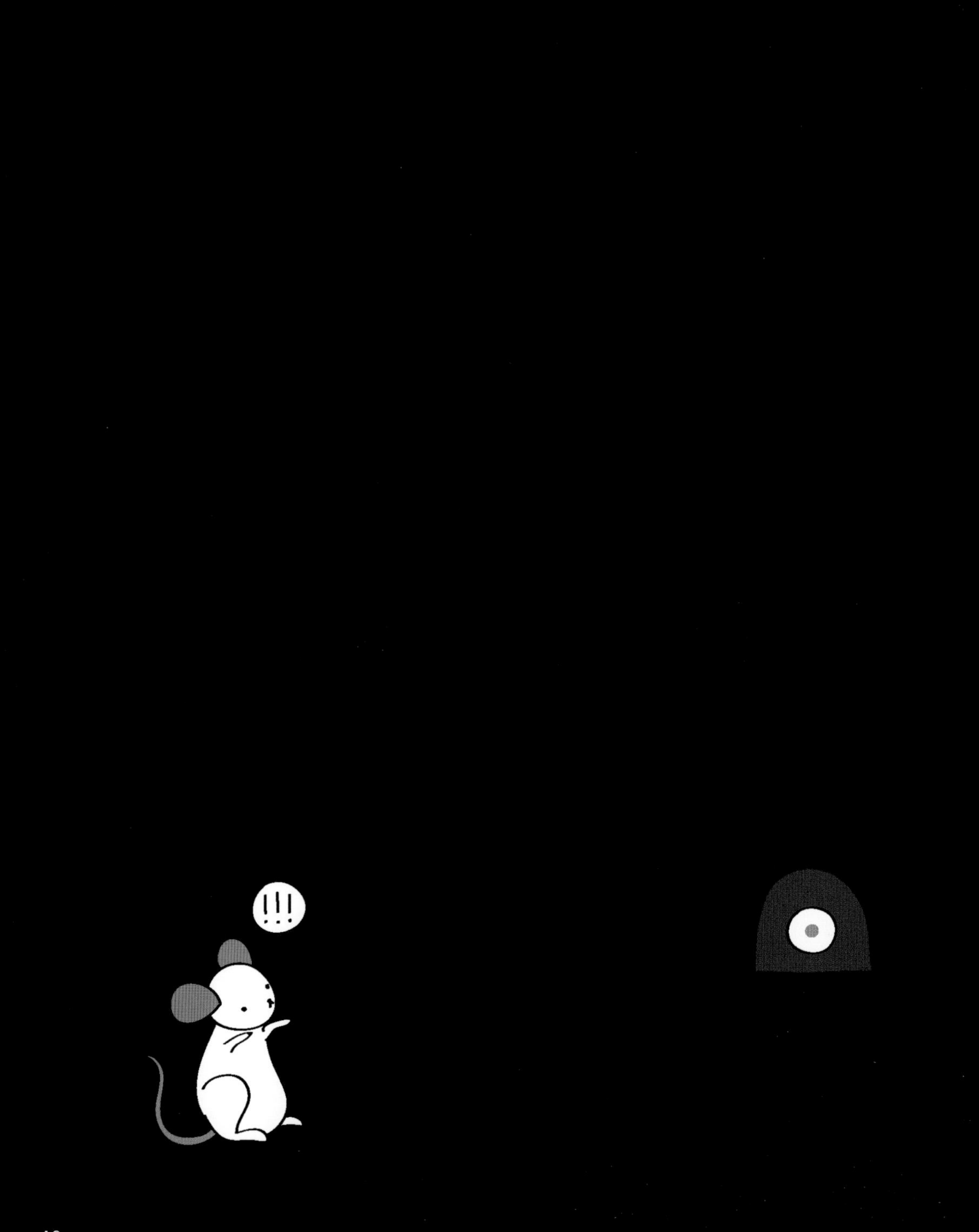
!!!

from **Pericles, Prince of Tyre**

William Shakespeare

"The cat, with eyne of burning coal,
Now crouches fore the mouse's hole."

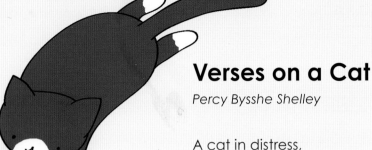

Verses on a Cat

Percy Bysshe Shelley

A cat in distress,
Nothing more, nor less;
Good folks, I must faithfully tell ye,
As I am a sinner,
It waits for some dinner
To stuff out its own little belly.

You would not easily guess
All the modes of distress
Which torture the tenants of earth;
And the various evils,
Which like so many devils,
Attend the poor souls from their birth.

Some a living require,
And others desire
An old fellow out of the way;
And which is the best

I leave to be guessed,
For I cannot pretend to say.

One wants society,
Another variety,
Others a tranquil life;
Some want food,
Others, as good,
Only want a wife.

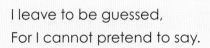

But this poor little cat
Only wanted a rat,
To stuff out its own little maw;
And it were as good
Some people had such food,
To make them *hold their jaw!*

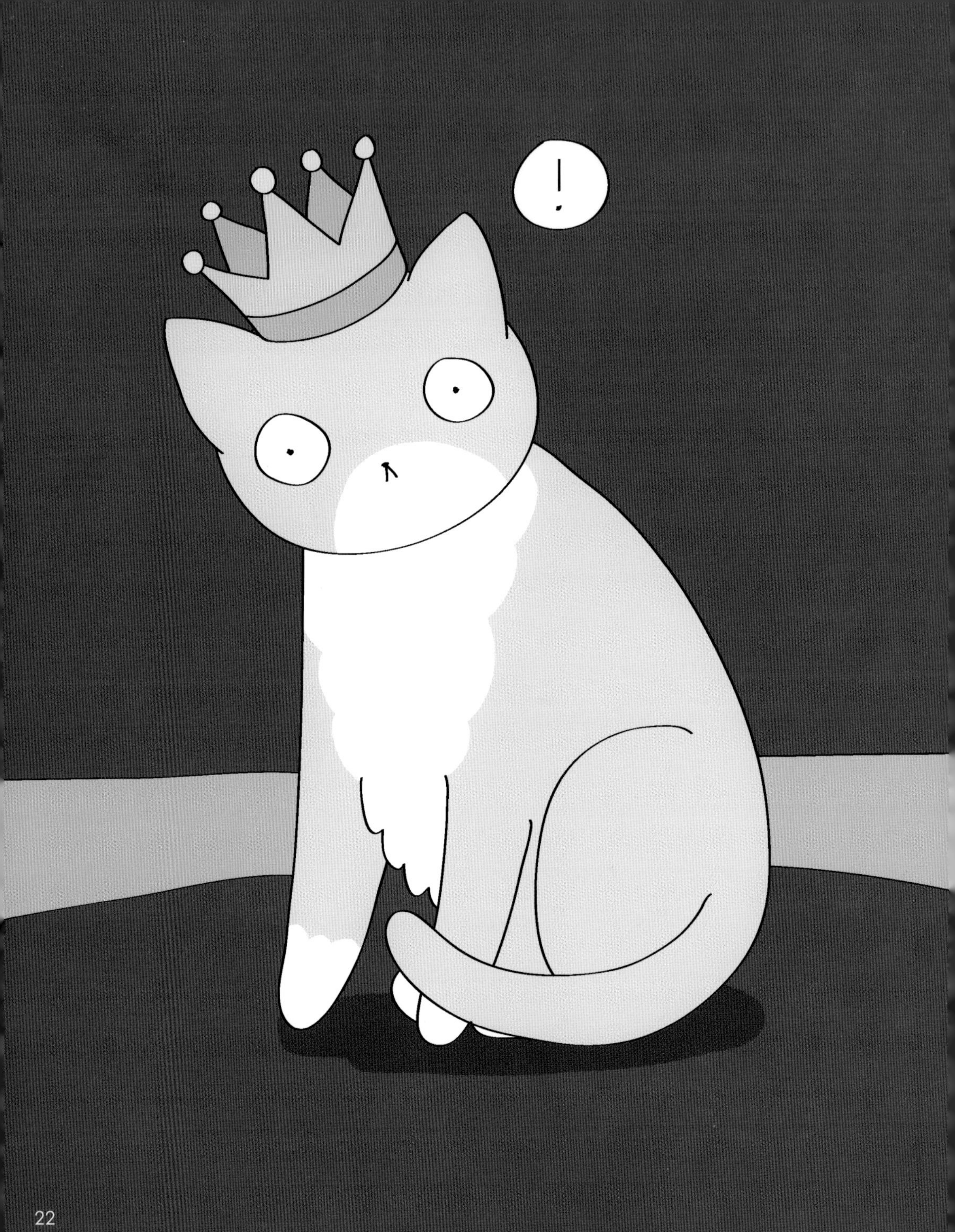
!

Pussy Cat, Pussy Cat

Pussy Cat, Pussy Cat, where have you been?
I've been to London to visit the Queen.
Pussy Cat, Pussy Cat, what did you there?
I frightened a little mouse under the chair.

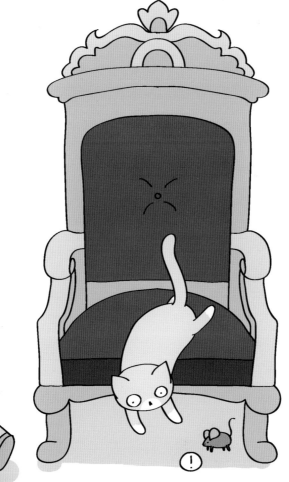

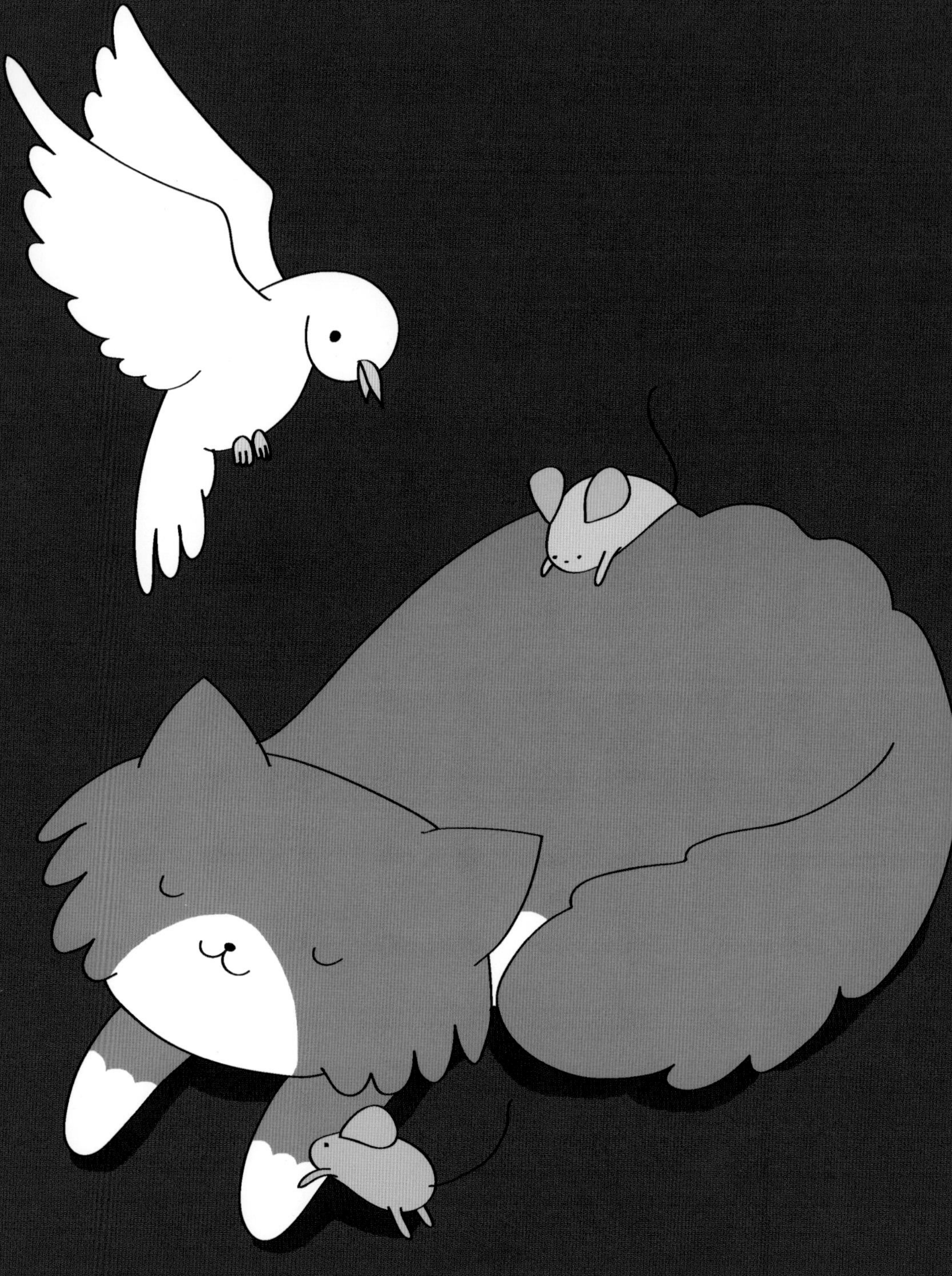

The Lazy Pussy

Palmer Cox

There lives a good-for-nothing cat,
    So lazy it appears,
That chirping birds can safely come
    And light upon her ears.

And rats and mice can venture out
    To nibble at her toes,
Or climb around and pull her tail,
    And boldly scratch her nose.

Fine servants brush her silken coat
    And give her cream for tea;—
Yet she's a good-for-nothing cat,
    As all the world may see.

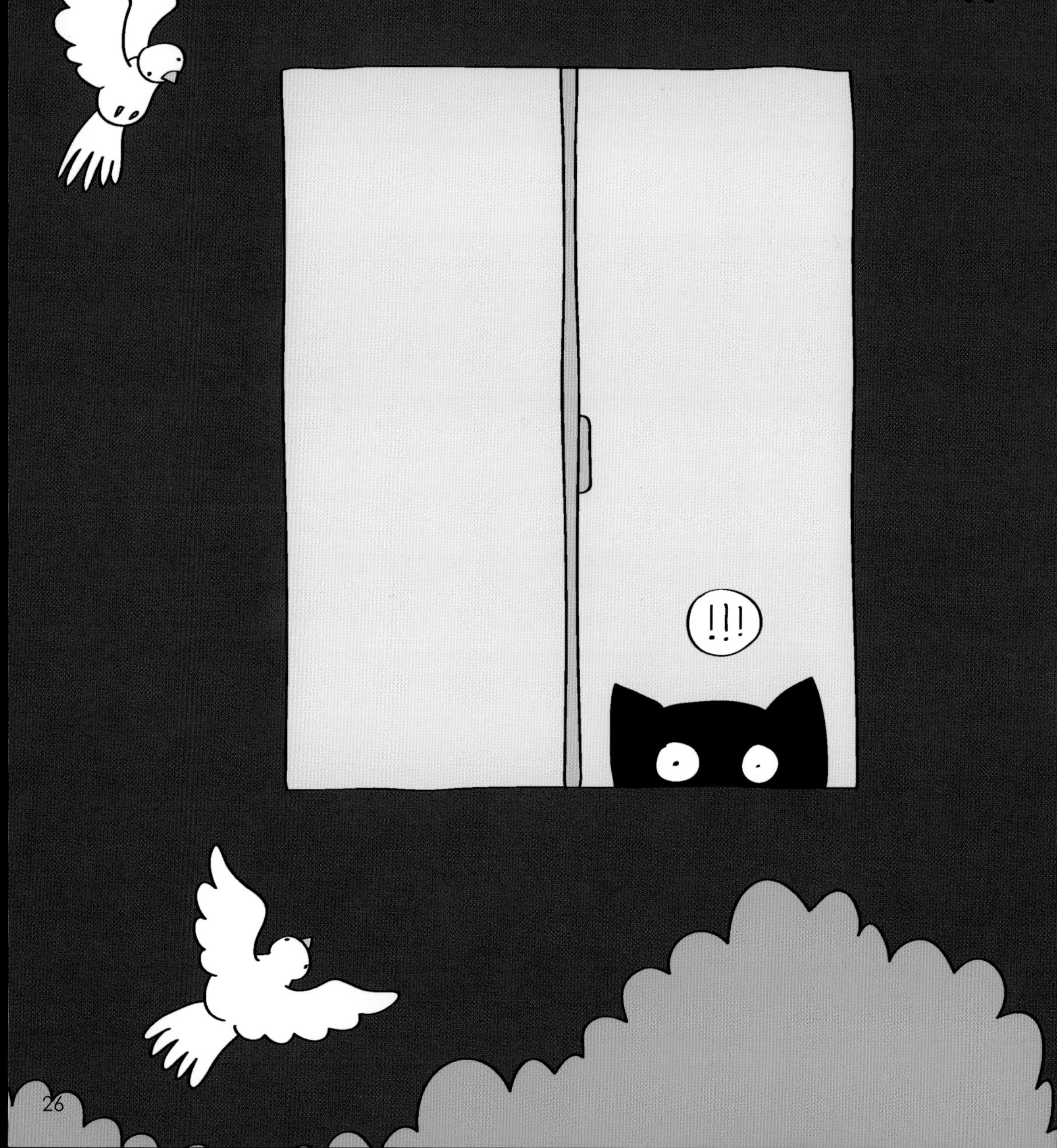
!!!

She Sights a Bird

Emily Dickinson

She sights a Bird—she chuckles—
She flattens—then she crawls—
She runs without the look of feet—
Her eyes increase to Balls—

Her Jaws stir—twitching—hungry—
Her Teeth can hardly stand—
She leaps, but Robin leaped the first—
Ah, Pussy, of the Sand,

The Hopes so juicy ripening—
You almost bathed your Tongue—
When Bliss disclosed a hundred Toes—
And fled with every one—

A Cat's Conscience

A dog will often steal a bone,
But conscience lets him not alone,
And by his tail his guilt is known.

But cats consider theft a game,
And, howsoever you may blame,
Refuse the slightest sign of shame.

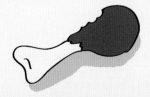

When food mysteriously goes,
The chances are that Pussy knows
More than she leads you to suppose.

And hence there is no need for you,
If Puss declines a meal or two,
To feel her pulse and make ado.

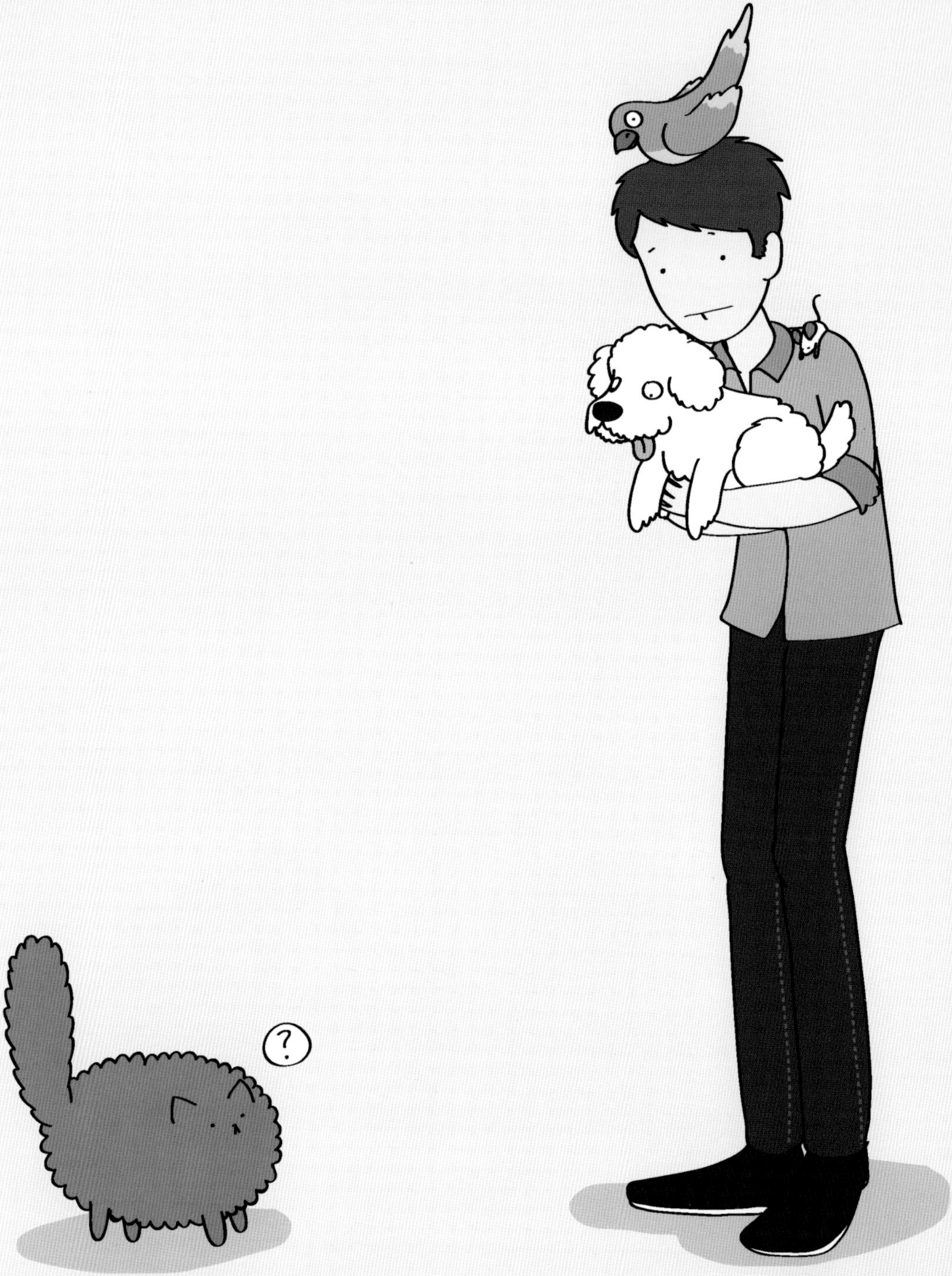
?

from **Sad Memories**

Charles Stuart Calverley

They tell me I am beautiful: they praise my silken hair,
My little feet that silently slip on from stair to stair:
They praise my pretty trustful face and innocent grey eye;
Fond hands caress me oftentimes, yet would that I might die!

Why was I born to be abhorr'd of man and bird and beast?
The bullfinch marks me stealing by, and
    straight his song hath ceased;
The shrewmouse eyes me shudderingly,
    then flees; and, worse than that,
The housedog he flees after me—why was I born a cat?

Men prize the heartless hound who quits
    dry-eyed his native land;
Who wags a mercenary tail and licks a tyrant hand.
The leal true cat they prize not, that if e'er compell'd to roam
Still flies, when let out of the bag, precipitately home.

They call me cruel. Do I know if mouse or song-bird feels?
I only know they make me light and salutary meals:
And if, as 'tis my nature to, ere I devour I tease 'em,
Why should a low-bred gardener's boy
    pursue me with a besom?

from **The Kitten and Falling Leaves**

William Wordsworth

That way look, my Infant, lo!
What a pretty baby-show!
See the Kitten on the wall,
Sporting with the leaves that fall,
Withered leaves—one—two—and three—
From the lofty elder-tree!
Through the calm and frosty air
Of this morning bright and fair,
Eddying round and round they sink
Softly, slowly: one might think
From the motions that are made,
Every little leaf conveyed
Sylph or Faery hither tending,—
To this lower world descending,
Each invisible and mute,
In his wavering parachute.

—But the Kitten, how she starts,
Crouches, stretches, paws, and darts!
First at one, and then its fellow
Just as light and just as yellow;
There are many now—now one—
Now they stop and there are none:
What intenseness of desire
In her upward eye of fire!
With a tiger-leap half-way
Now she meets the coming prey,
Lets it go as fast, and then
Has it in her power again:
Now she works with three or four,
Like an Indian conjurer;
Quick as he in feats of art,
Far beyond in joy of heart.

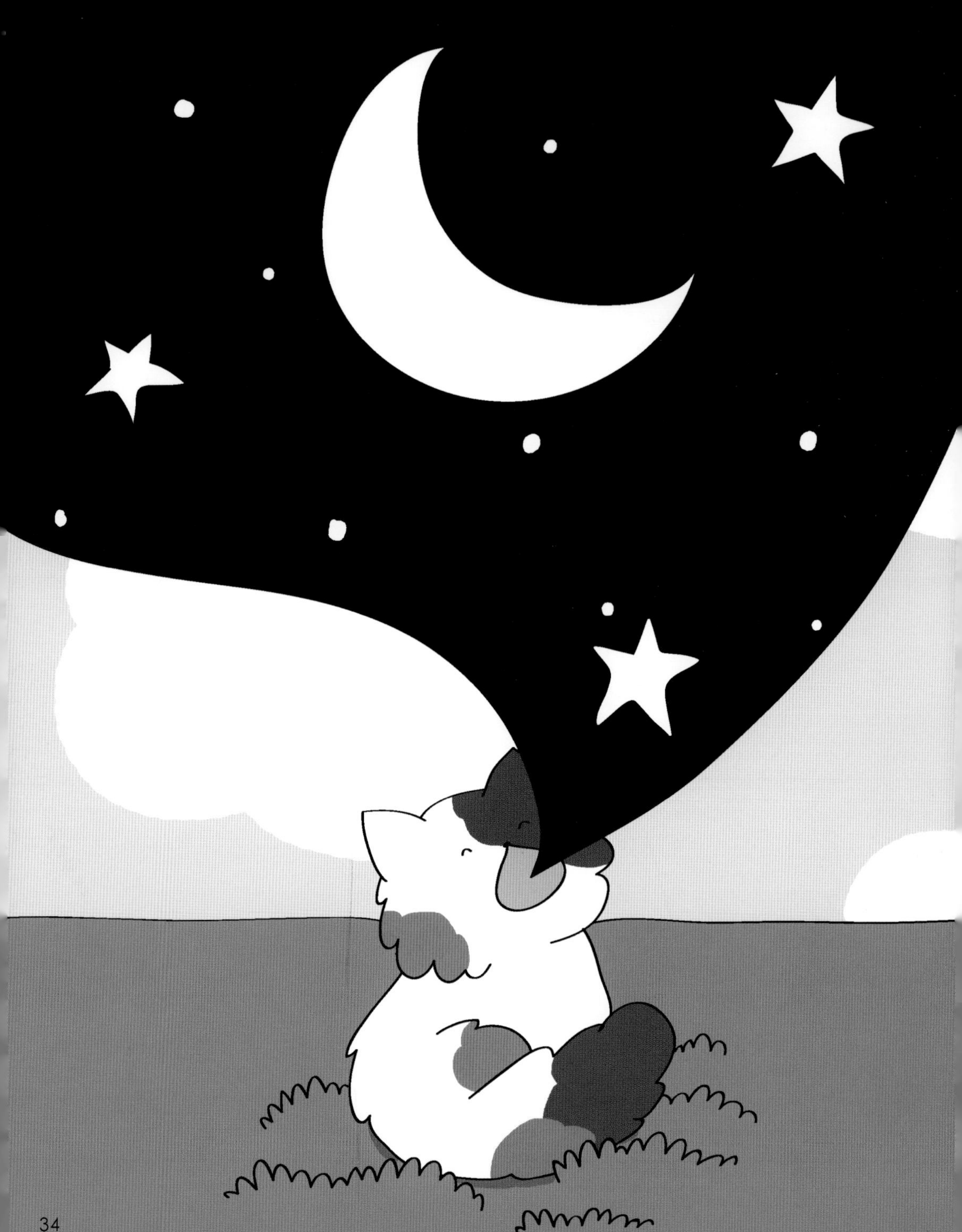

Dawn

The little kitten's face
Like the sudden dawn
Swallows all of midnight
With a big pink yawn.

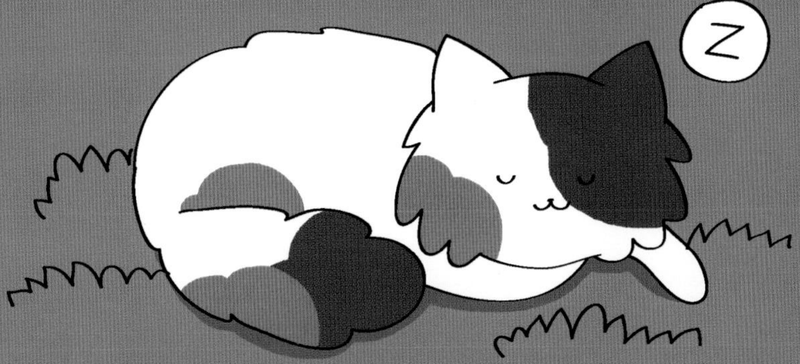
Z

from **Three Little Kittens**

Eliza Lee Follen

Three little kittens lost their mittens;
And they began to cry,
"Oh, Mother dear, we very much fear
our mittens we have lost."

"What! Lost your mittens, you naughty kittens!
Then you shall have no pie."
"Mee-ow, mee-ow, mee-ow, mee-ow."
"No, you shall have no pie."

The three little kittens they found their mittens;
And they began to cry,
"Oh, Mother dear, see here, see here!
Our mittens we have found."

"What! Found your mittens! You good little kittens,
Now you shall have some pie!"
"Purr, purr, purr, purr,
Purr, purr, purr."

from **The Kitten**

Joanna Baillie

Wanton drole, whose harmless play
Beguiles the rustic's closing day,
When drawn the evening fire about,
Sit aged crone and thoughtless lout,
And child upon his three-foot stool,
Waiting till his supper cool;
And maid, whose cheek outblooms the rose,
As bright the blazing faggot glows,
Who, bending to the friendly light,
Plies her task with busy sleight;
Come, show thy tricks and sportive graces,
Thus circled round with merry faces.

Backward coil'd and crouching low,
With glaring eyeballs watch thy foe,
The housewife's spindle whirling round,
Or thread, or straw, that on the ground
Its shadow throws, by urchin sly
Held out to lure thy roving eye;
Then, onward stealing, fiercely spring
Upon the futile, faithless thing.
Now, wheeling round, with bootless skill,
Thy bo-peep tail provokes thee still,
As still beyond thy curving side
Its jetty tip is seen to glide;
Till, from thy centre starting far,
Thou sidelong rear'st with rump in air,
Erected stiff, and gait awry,
Like madam in her tantrums high:
Tho' ne'er a madam of them all
Whose silken kirtle sweeps the hall,
More varied trick and whim displays
To catch the admiring stranger's gaze.

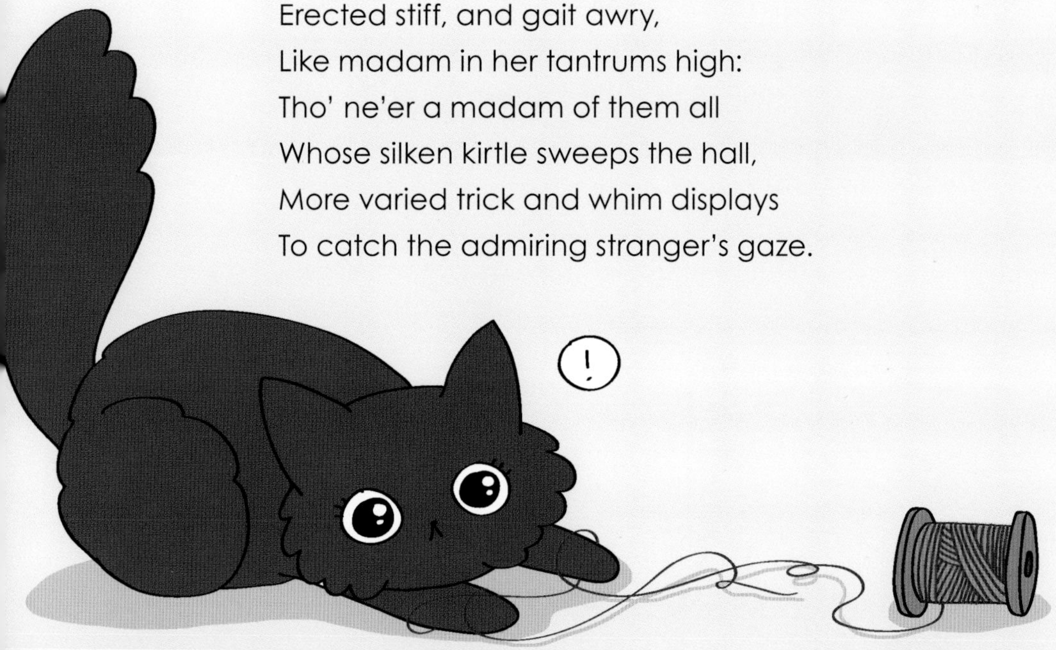
!

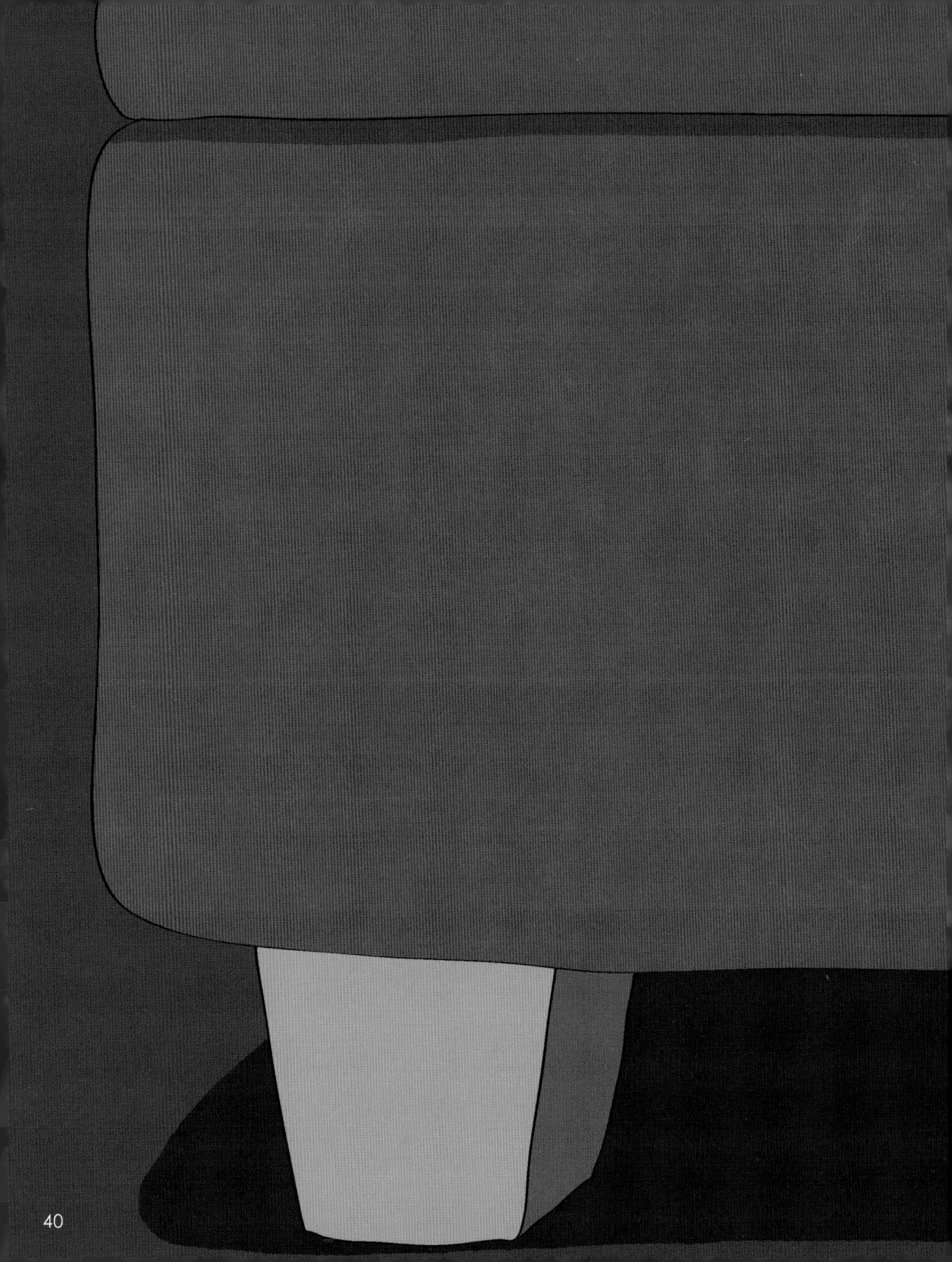

Sonnet to a Cat

John Keats

Cat! who hast pass'd thy grand climacteric,
How many mice and rats hast in thy days
Destroy'd? —How many tit bits stolen? Gaze
With those bright languid segments green, and prick
Those velvet ears—but pr'ythee do not stick
Thy latent talons in me—and upraise
Thy gentle mew—and tell me all thy frays
Of fish and mice, and rats and tender chick.
Nay, look not down, nor lick thy dainty wrists—
For all the wheezy asthma,—and for all
Thy tail's tip is nick'd off—and though the fists
Of many a maid have given thee many a maul,
Still is that fur as soft as when the lists
In youth thou enter'dst on glass bottled wall.

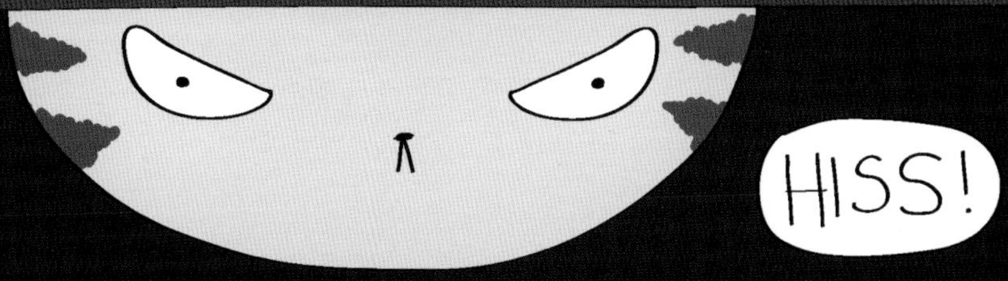
HISS!

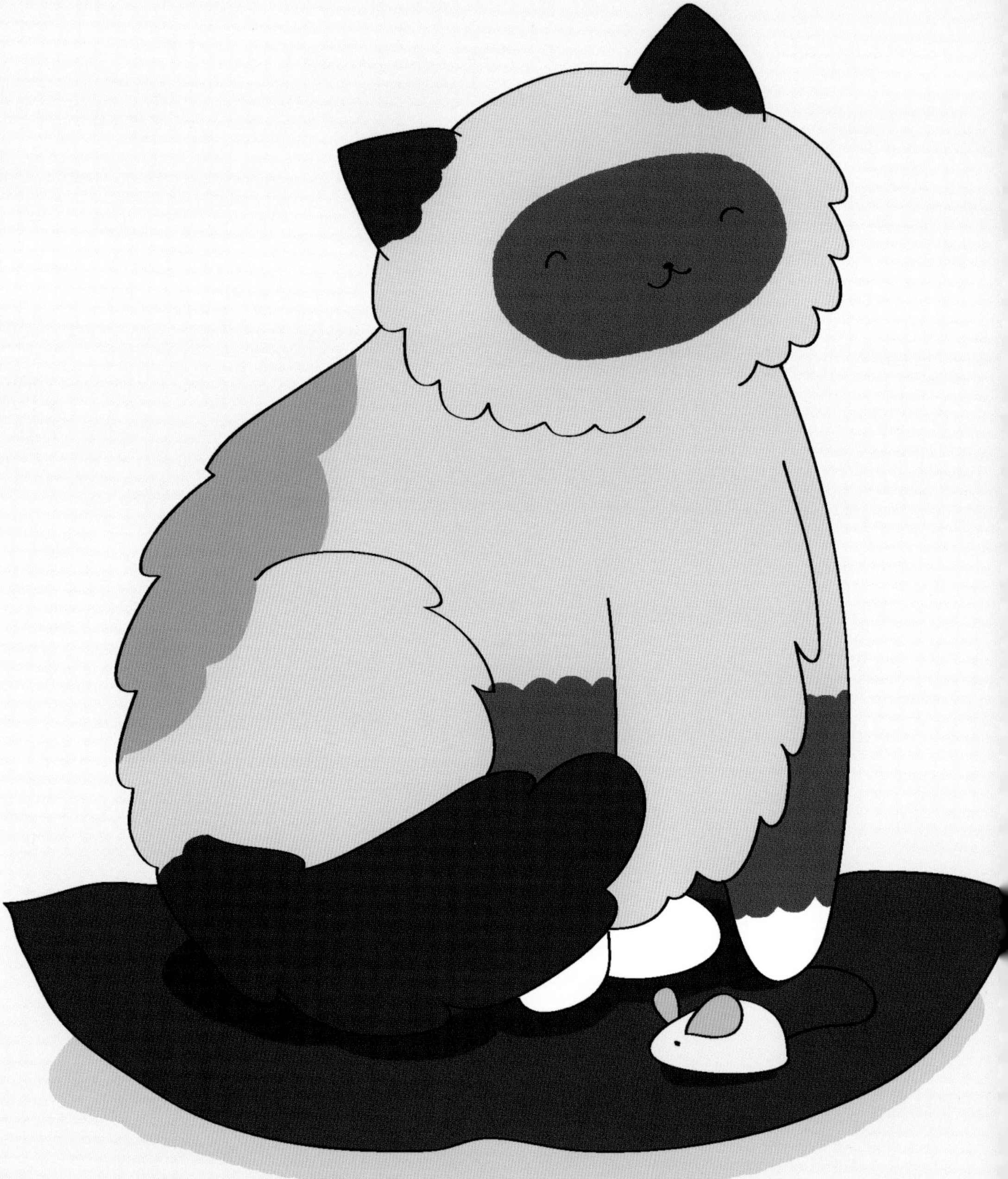

Montague Michael

Montague Michael
You're much too fat,
You wicked old, wily old,
Well-fed cat.

All night you sleep
On a cushion of silk,
And twice a day
I bring you milk.

And once in a while,
When you catch a mouse,
You're the proudest person
In all the house.

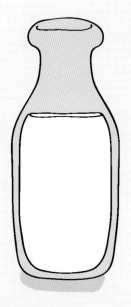

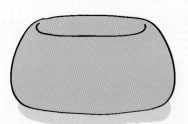

On the Death of a Cat,
A Friend of Mine
Aged Ten Years and a Half

Christina Rossetti

Who shall tell the lady's grief
When her cat was past relief?
Who shall number the hot tears
Shed o'er her, belov'd for years?
Who shall say the dark dismay
Which her dying caused that day?

Come, ye Muses, one and all,
Come obedient to my call;
Come and mourn with tuneful breath
Each one for a separate death;
And, while you in numbers sigh,
I will sing her elegy.

Of a noble race she came,
And Grimalkin was her name.
Young and old full many a mouse
Felt the prowess of her house;
Weak and strong full many a rat
Cowered beneath her crushing pat;
And the birds around the place
Shrank from her too close embrace.
But one night, reft of her strength,
She lay down and died at length:
Lay a kitten by her side
In whose life the mother died.
Spare her line and lineage,
Guard her kitten's tender age,
And that kitten's name as wide
Shall be known as hers that died.
And whoever passes by
The poor grave where Puss doth lie,
Softly, softly let him tread,
Nor disturb her narrow bed.

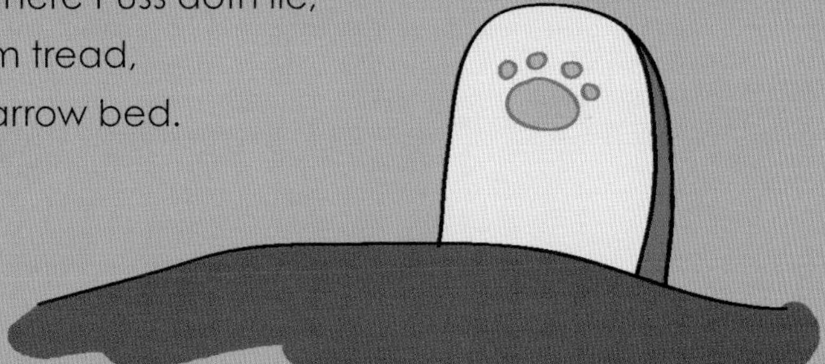

I Love Little Pussy

I love little Pussy, her coat is so warm;
And if I don't hurt her she'll do me no harm.
So I'll not pull her tail, nor drive her away,
But Pussy and I very gently will play.

She shall sit by my side, and I'll give her some food;
And she'll love me because I am gentle and good.
I'll pat little Pussy and then she will purr,
And thus show her thanks for my kindness to her.

I'll not pinch her ears, nor tread on her paw,
Lest I should provoke her to use her sharp claw;
I never will vex her, nor make her displeased,
For Pussy can't bear to be worried or teased.

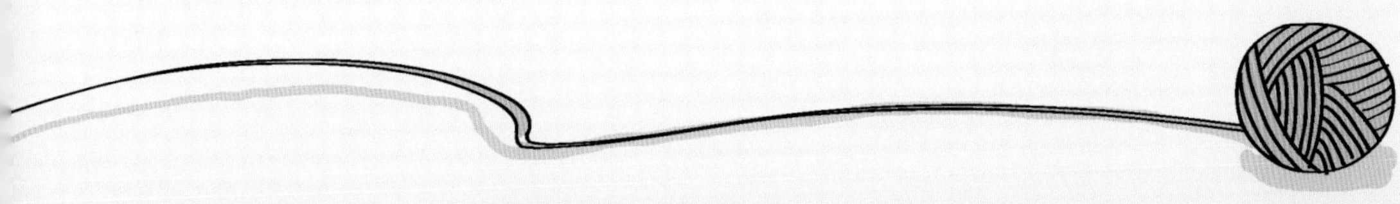

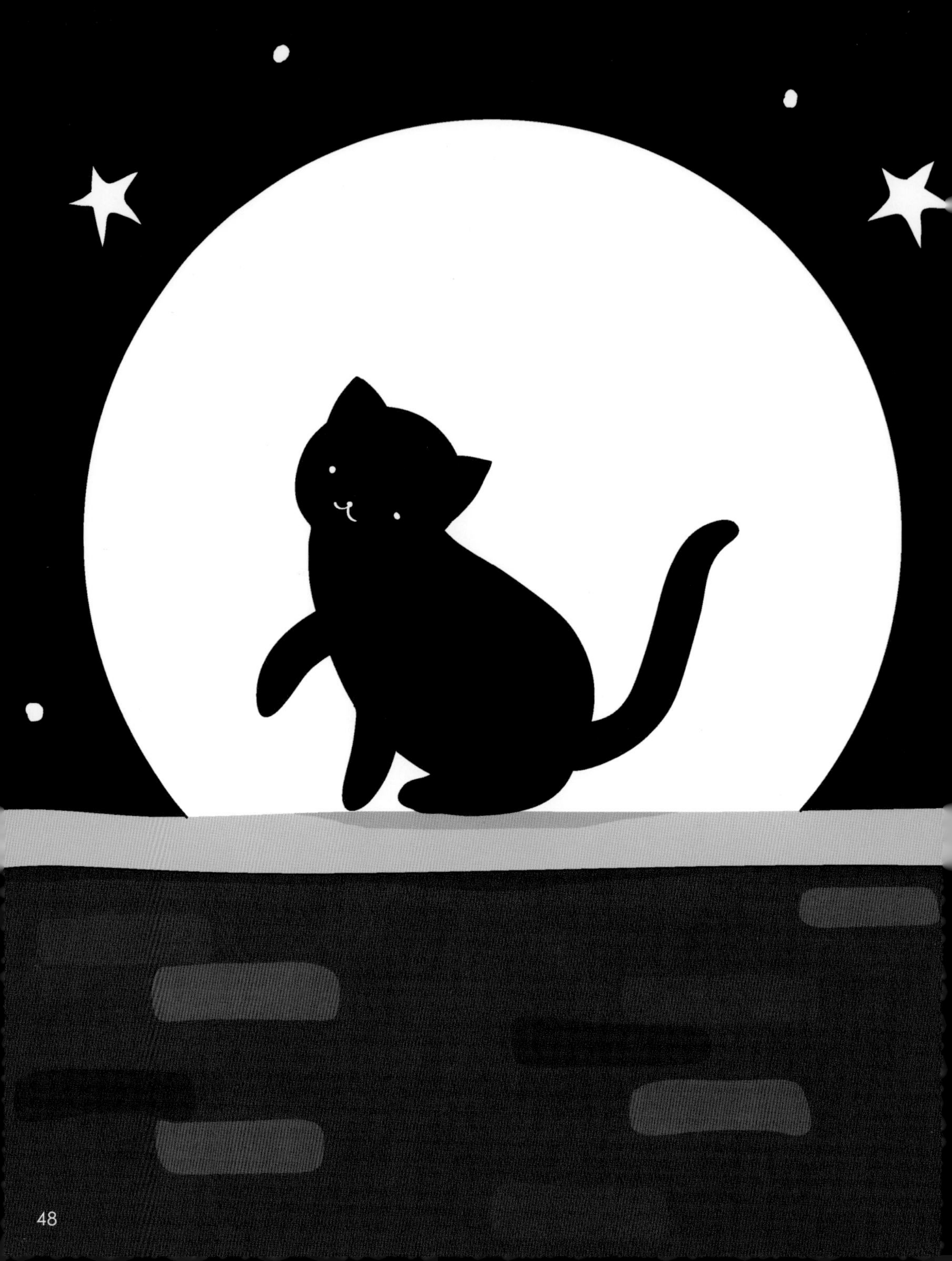

The Cat of Cats

William Brighty Rands

I am the cat of cats. I am
The everlasting cat!
Cunning, and old, and sleek as jam,
The everlasting cat!
I hunt vermin in the night—
The everlasting cat!
For I see best without the light—
The everlasting cat!

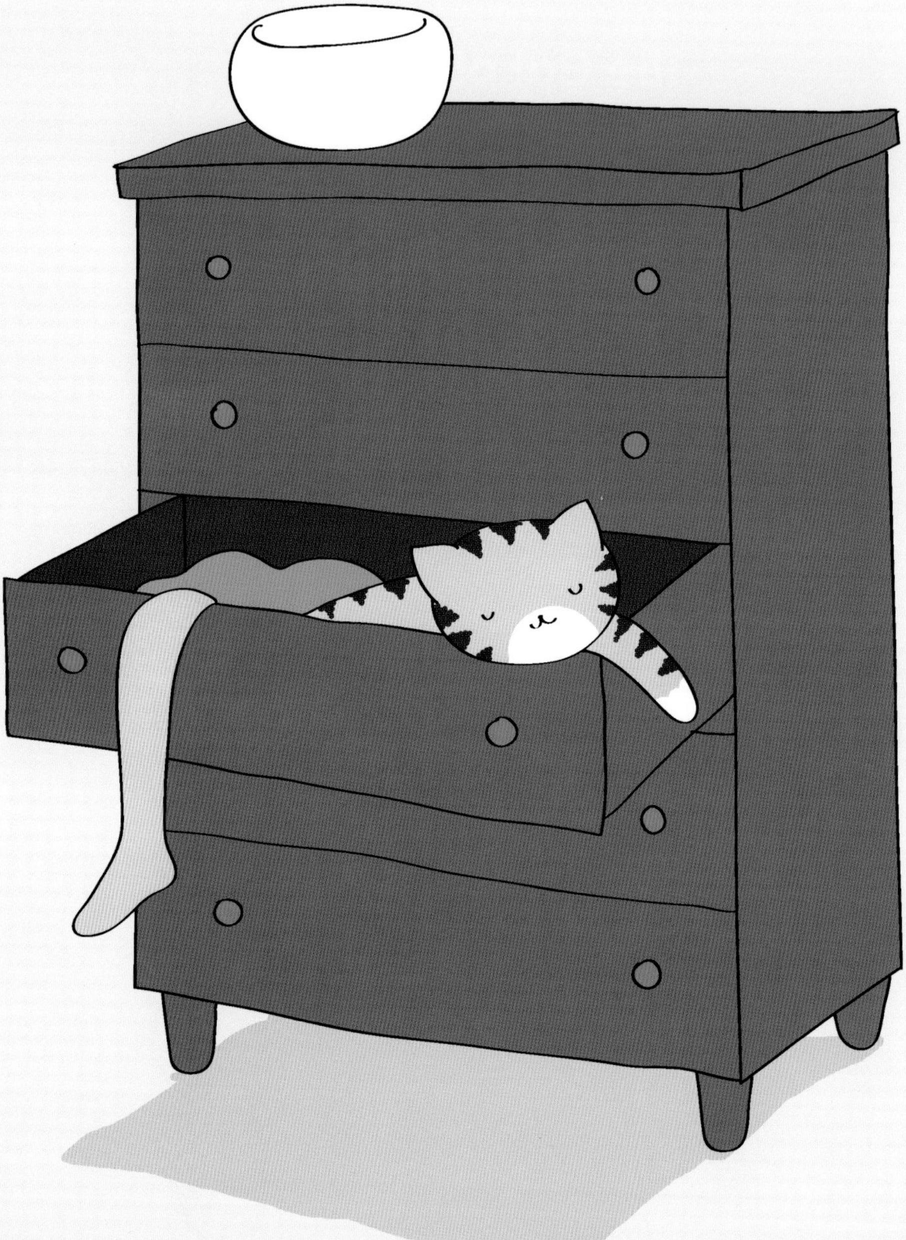

from **The Retired Cat**

William Cowper

A poet's cat, sedate and grave
As poet well could wish to have,
Was much addicted to inquire
For nooks to which she might retire,
And where, secure as mouse in chink,
She might repose or sit and think. . . .
A drawer, it chanc'd, at bottom lin'd,
With linen of the softest kind,
With such as merchants introduce
From India, for the ladies' use—
A drawer, impending o'er the rest,
Half-open in the topmost chest,
Of depth enough, and none to spare,
Invited her to slumber there;
Puss with delight beyond expression,
Survey'd the scene, and took possession.

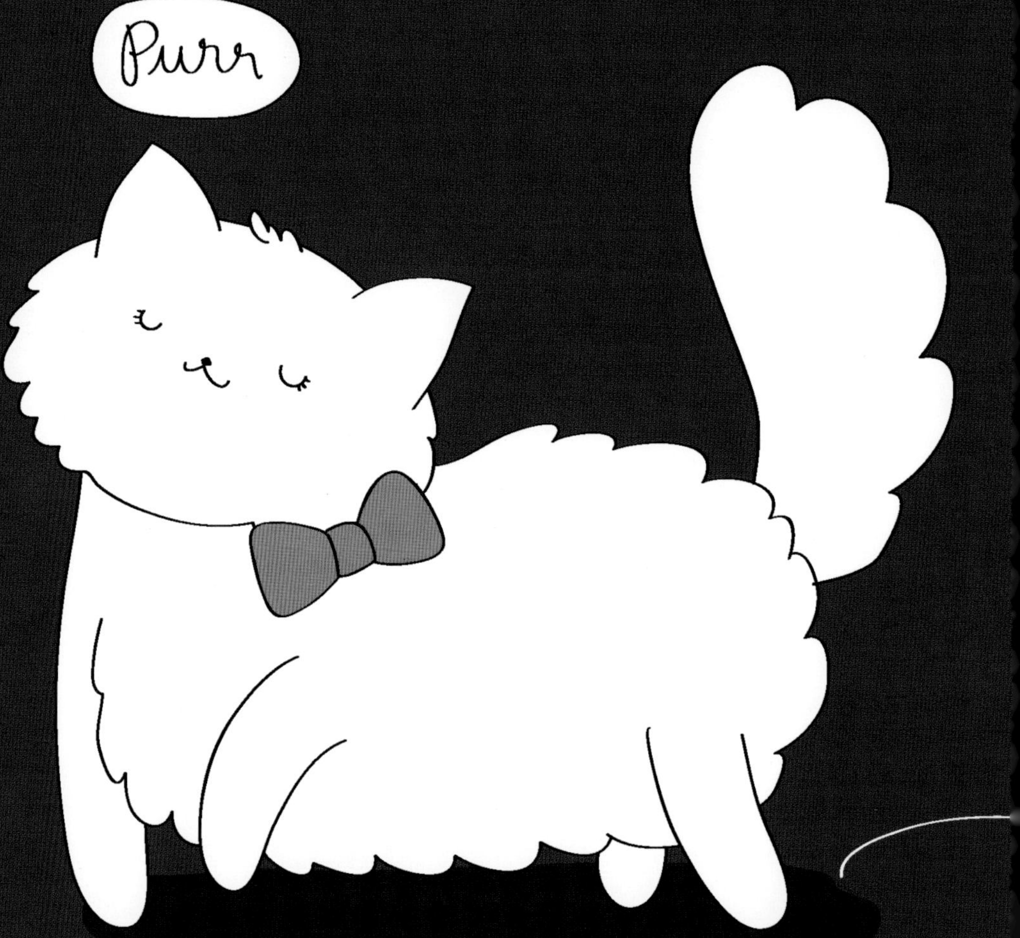
Purr

To a Persian Cat

F. C. W. Hiley

So dear, so dainty, so demure,
So charming in whate'er position;
By race the purest of the pure,
A little cat of high condition:
Her coat lies not in trim-kept rows
Of carpet-like and vulgar sleekness:
But like a ruffled sea it grows
Of wavy grey (my special weakness):
She vexes not the night with squalls
That make one seize a boot and throw it:
She joins in no unseemly brawls
(At least she never lets me know it!):
She never bursts in at the door
In manner boisterous and loud:
But silently along the floor
She passes, like a little cloud.
Then, opening wide her amber eyes,
Puts an inquiring nose up—
Sudden upon my knee she flies,
Then purrs and tucks her little toes up.

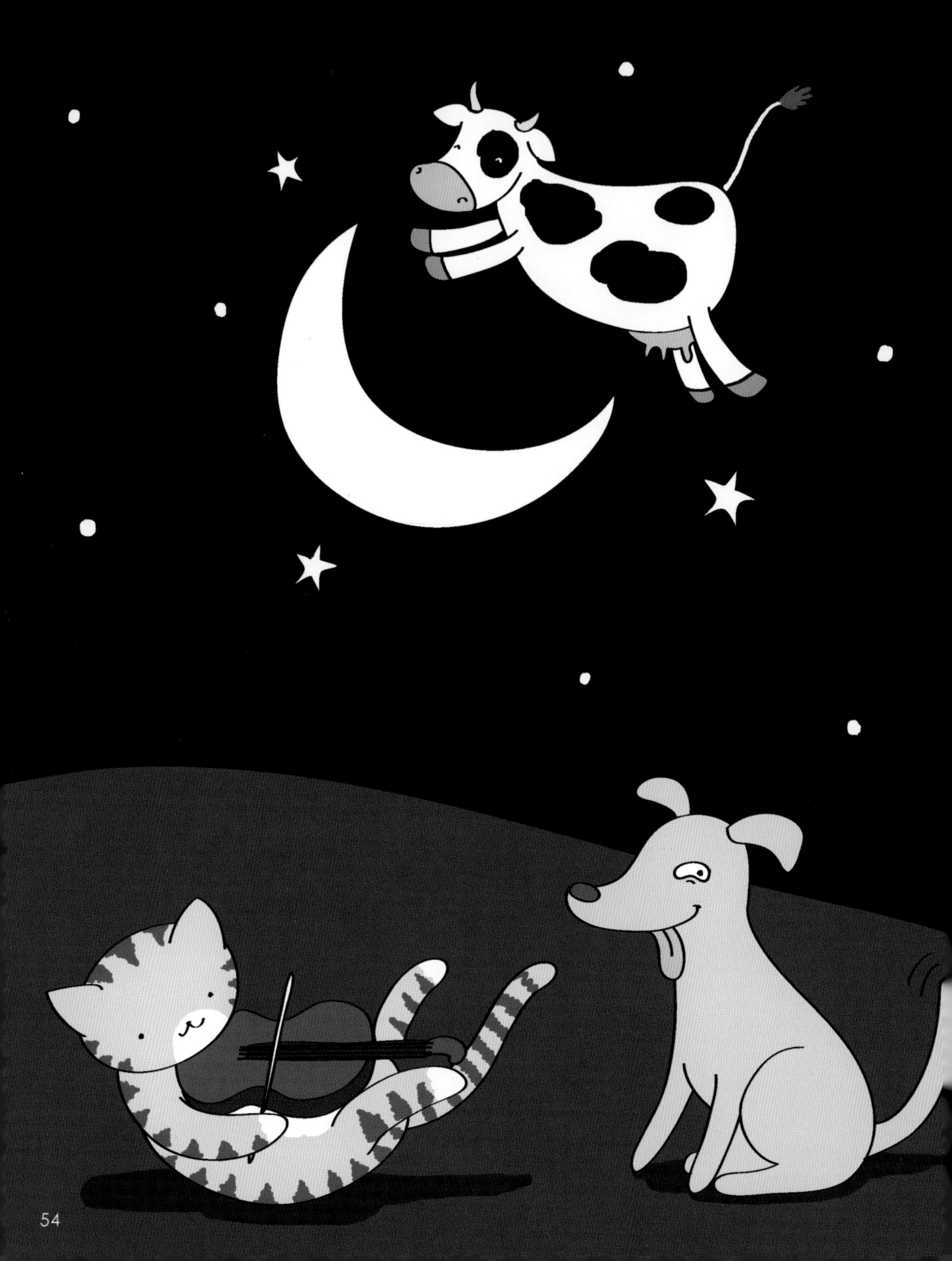

Hey, Diddle, Diddle

Hey, diddle, diddle,
The cat and the fiddle,
The cow jumped over the moon;
The little dog laughed
To see such sport,
And the dish ran away with the spoon.

The Duel

Eugene Field

The gingham dog and the calico cat
Side by side on the table sat;
'T was half-past twelve, and (what do you think!)
Nor one nor t' other had slept a wink!
The old Dutch clock and the Chinese plate
Appeared to know as sure as fate
There was going to be a terrible spat.
(I wasn't there; I simply state
What was told to me by the Chinese plate!)

The gingham dog went "Bow-wow-wow!"
And the calico cat replied "Mee-ow!"
The air was littered, an hour or so,
With bits of gingham and calico,
While the old Dutch clock in the chimney-place
Up with its hands before its face,
For it always dreaded a family row!
(Now mind: I'm only telling you
What the old Dutch clock declares is true!)

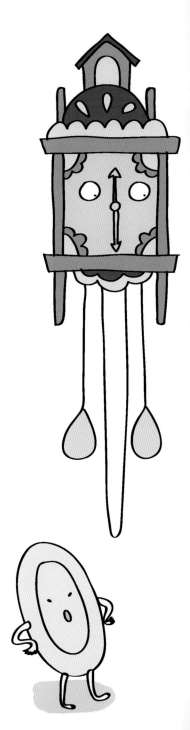

The Chinese plate looked very blue,
And wailed, "Oh, dear! what shall we do!"
But the gingham dog and the calico cat
Wallowed this way and tumbled that,
Employing every tooth and claw
In the awfullest way you ever saw—
And, oh! how the gingham and calico flew!
(Don't fancy I exaggerate—
I got my news from the Chinese plate!)

Next morning, where the two had sat
They found no trace of dog or cat;
And some folks think unto this day
That burglars stole that pair away!
But the truth about the cat and pup
Is this: they ate each other up!
Now what do you really think of that!
(The old Dutch clock it told me so,
And that is how I came to know.)

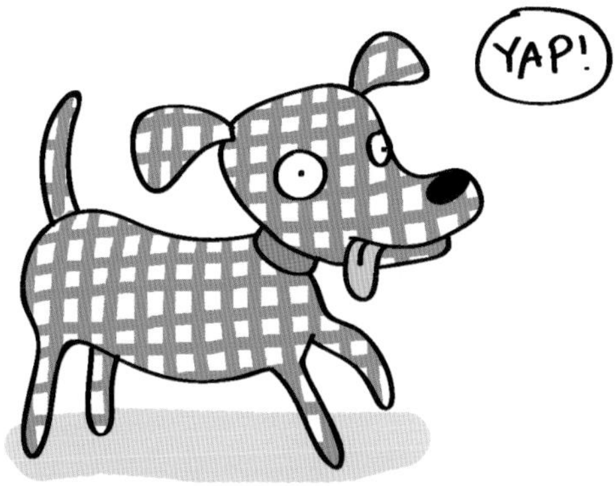
YAP!

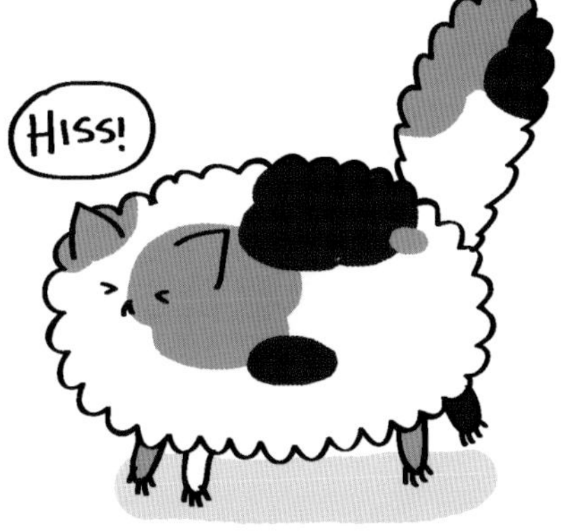
HISS!

from **Old Dame Trot and Her Comical Cat**

Dame Trot and her Cat
Sat down for a chat;
The Dame sat on this side,
And Puss sat on that.

The Dame went to market
To buy her a mouse;
When she came back
Puss was sweeping the house.

She went for some ale,
Because she was dry;
When she came back,
Puss was making a pye.

She went out to buy
Miss Puss a new frock;
When she came back
She was riding poor Shock.

She went to buy apples,
And sugar and spice;
When she came back,
Puss was fiddling to mice.

She went out to buy
The Cat a new wig;
When she came back,
Puss was roasting a pig.

from **Jubilate Agno**

Christopher Smart

For I will consider my Cat Jeoffry . . .
For in his morning orisons he loves the
    sun and the sun loves him.
For he is of the tribe of Tiger.
For the Cherub Cat is a term of the Angel Tiger.
For he has the subtlety and hissing of a serpent,
    which in goodness he suppresses.
For he will not do destruction, if he is well-fed,
    neither will he spit without provocation.
For he purrs in thankfulness, when God
    tells him he's a good Cat.
For he is an instrument for the children
    to learn benevolence upon.
For every house is incomplete without him
    and a blessing is lacking in the spirit.

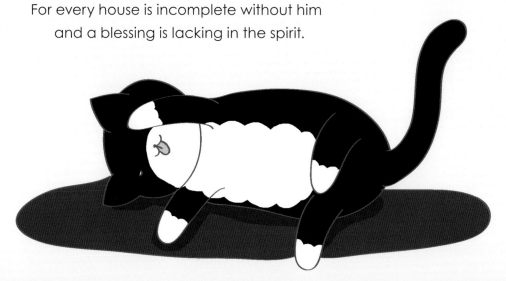

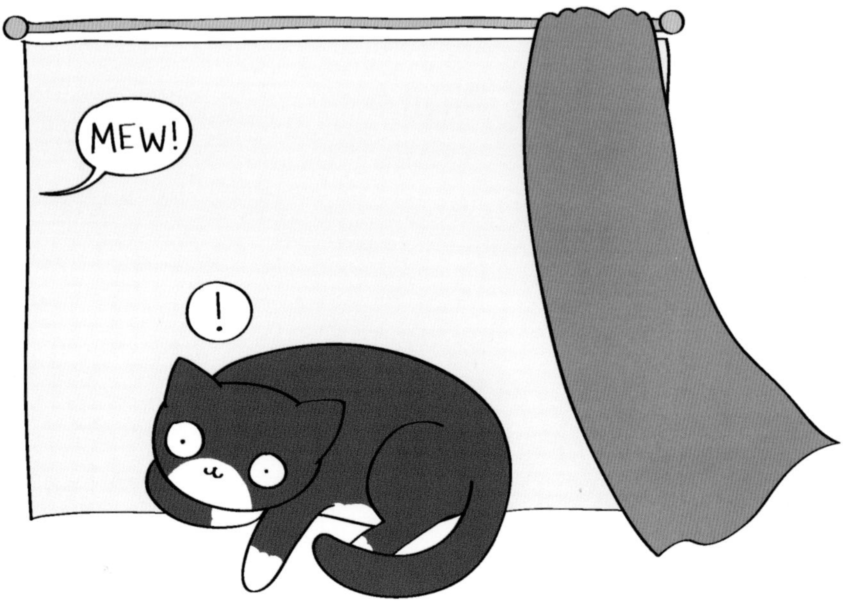
MEW!
!

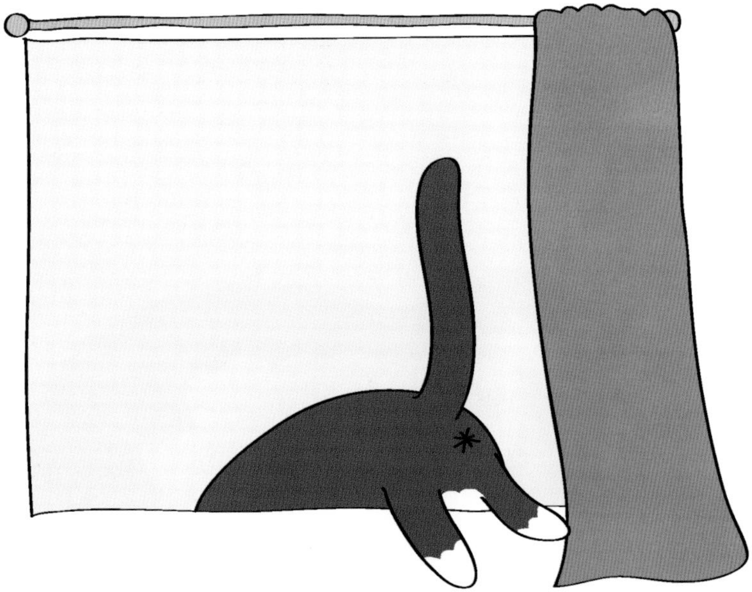

Having slept, the cat gets up

Kobayashi Issa

Having slept, the cat gets up,
yawns, goes out
to make love.

The Little Cat Angel

Leontine Stansfield

The ghost of a little white kitten
Crying mournfully, early and late,
Distracted St. Peter, the watchman,
As he guarded the heavenly gate.
"Say, what do you mean," said his saintship,
"Coming here and behaving like that?"
"I want to see Nellie, my missus,"
Sobbed the wee little ghost of a cat.
"I know she's not happy without me,
Won't you open and let me go in?"
"Begone," gasped the horrified watchman,
"Why the very idea is a sin;
I open the gate to good angels,
Not to stray little beggars like you."
"All right," mewed the little white kitten,
"Though a cat I'm a good angel, too."
Amazed at so bold an assertion,
But aware that he must make no mistake,
In silence, St. Peter long pondered,
For his name and repute were at stake,
Then placing the cat in his bosom
With a "Whist now, and say all your prayers,"
He opened the heavenly portals
And ascended the bright golden stairs.

A little girl angel came flying,
"That's my kitty, St. Peter," she cried.
And, seeing the joy of their meeting,
Peter let the angel cat abide.

This tale is the tale of a kitten
Dwelling now with the blessed above,
It vanquished grim Death and High Heaven,
For the name of the kitten was Love.

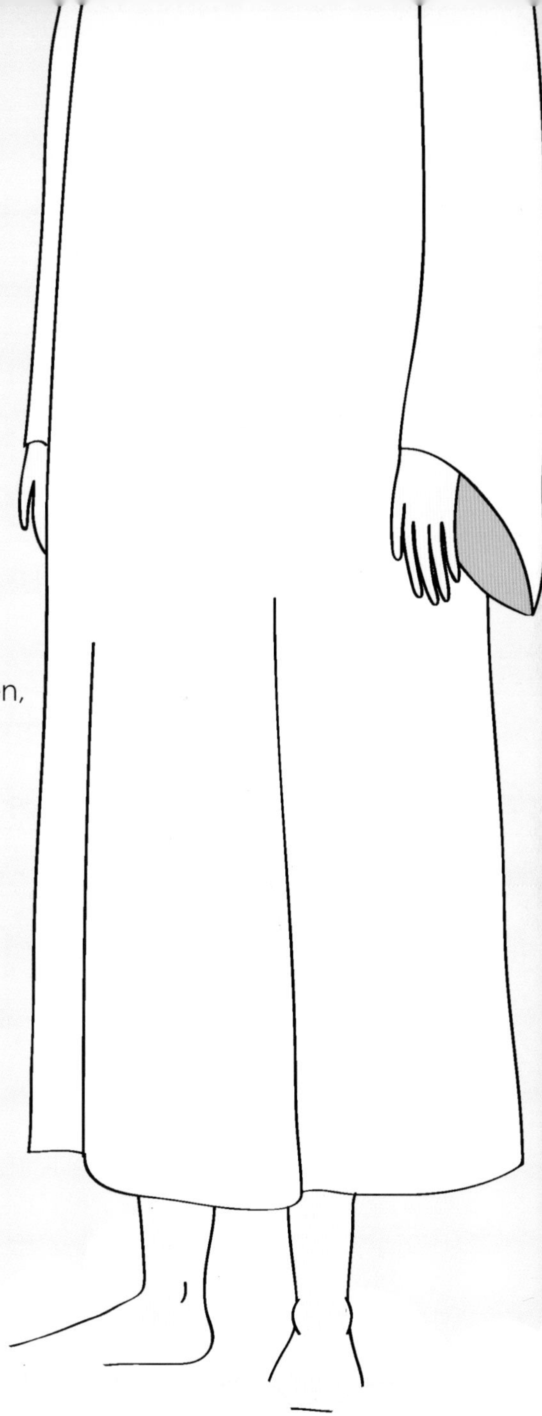

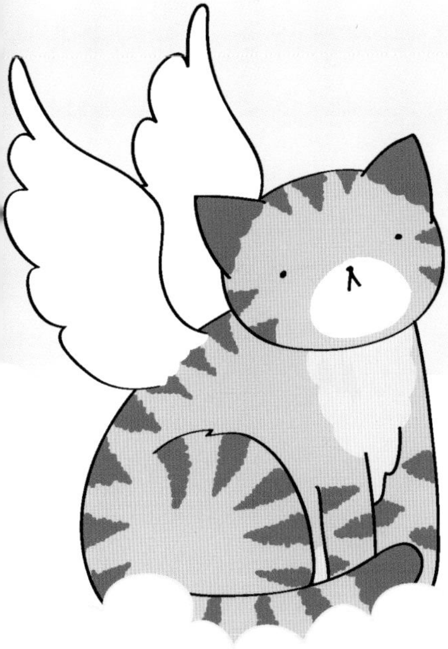

A Cat Came Fiddling

A cat came fiddling out of a barn,
With a pair of bagpipes under her arm;
She could sing nothing but fiddle-cum-fee
The mouse has married the bumblebee.
Pipe, cat; dance, mouse;
We'll have a wedding at our good house.

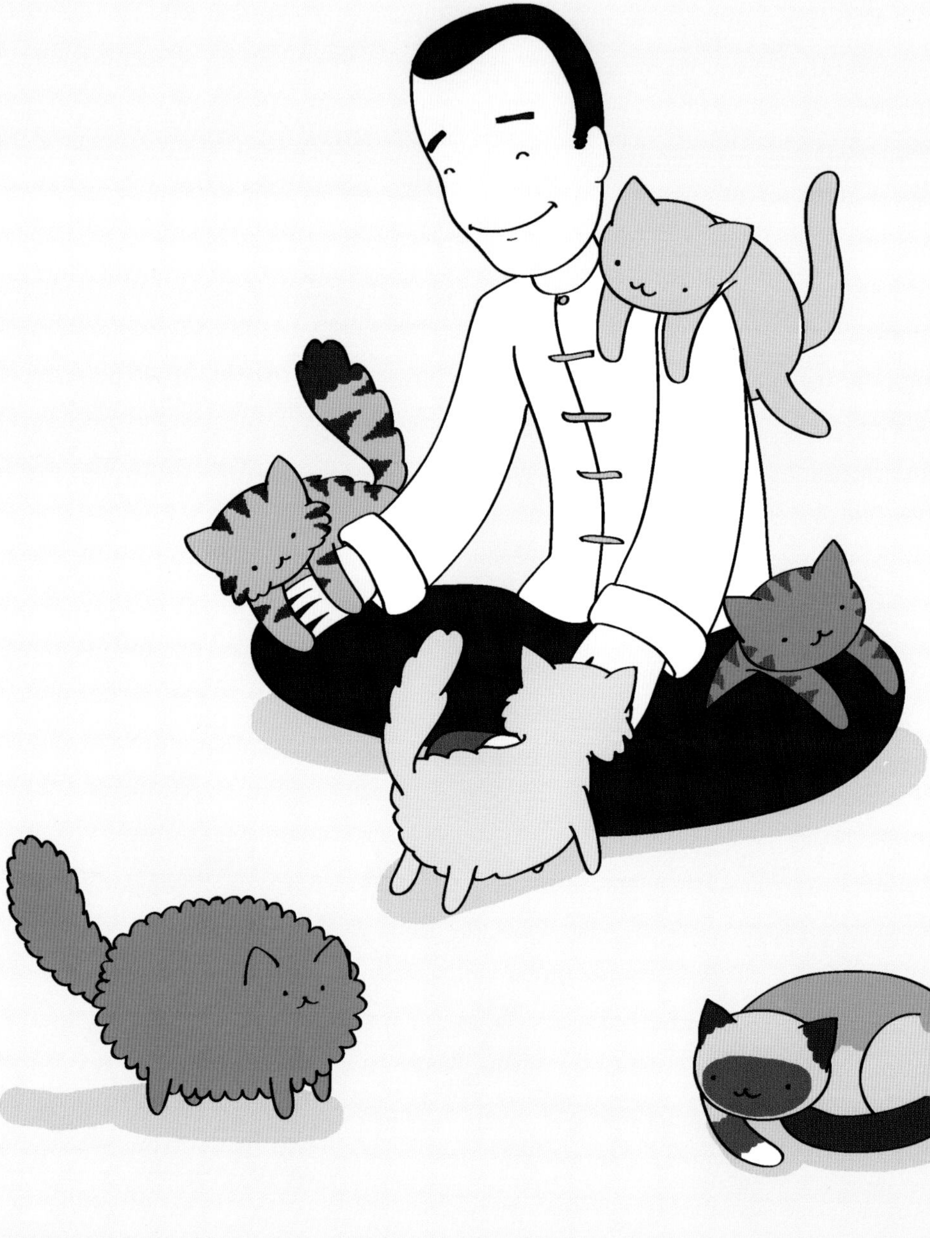

Chang Tuan's Cats

Wang Chih

Scholar Chang Tuan was fond of cats,
And had seven of them,
Wonderful beasts with wonderful names,

They were:

Guardian of the East
White Phoenix
Purple Blossom
Drive-Away-Vexation
Brocade Sash
Cloud Pattern
Ten Thousand Strings of Cash

Each was worth several pieces of gold,
And nothing could persuade Chang
To part with them.

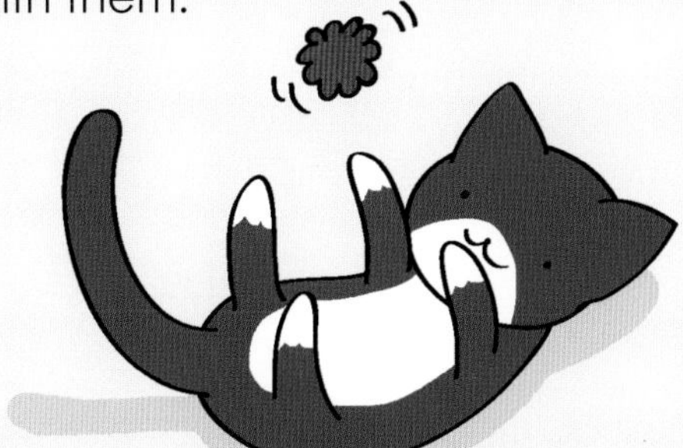

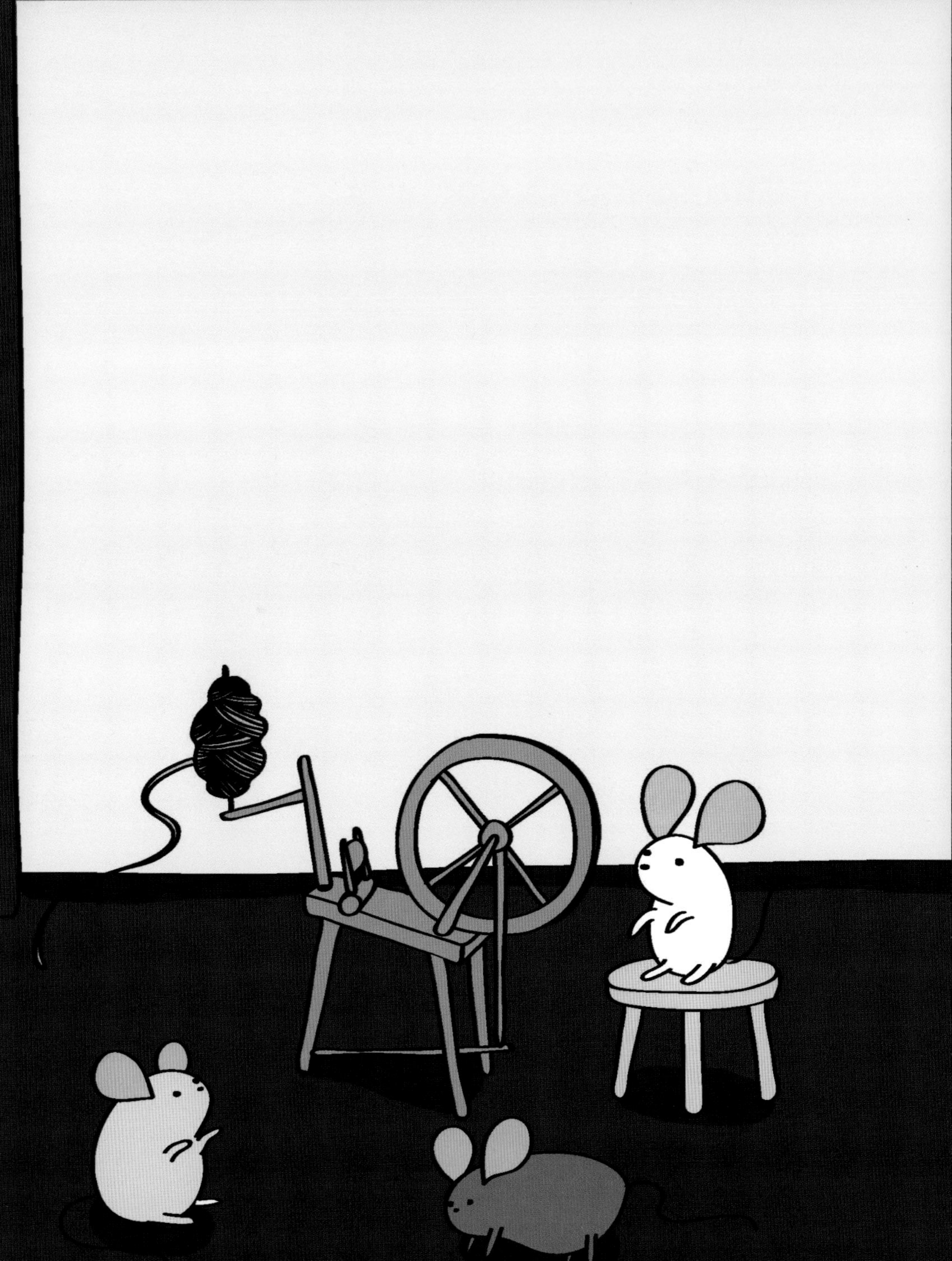

Six Little Mice Sat Down to Spin

Six little mice sat down to spin;
Pussy passed by and she peeped in;
"What are you doing, my little men?"
"Weaving coats for gentlemen."
"Shall I come in and cut off your threads?"
"No, no, Mistress Pussy, you'd bite off our heads."
"Oh, no, I'll not; I'll help you spin."
"That may be so, but you don't come in!"

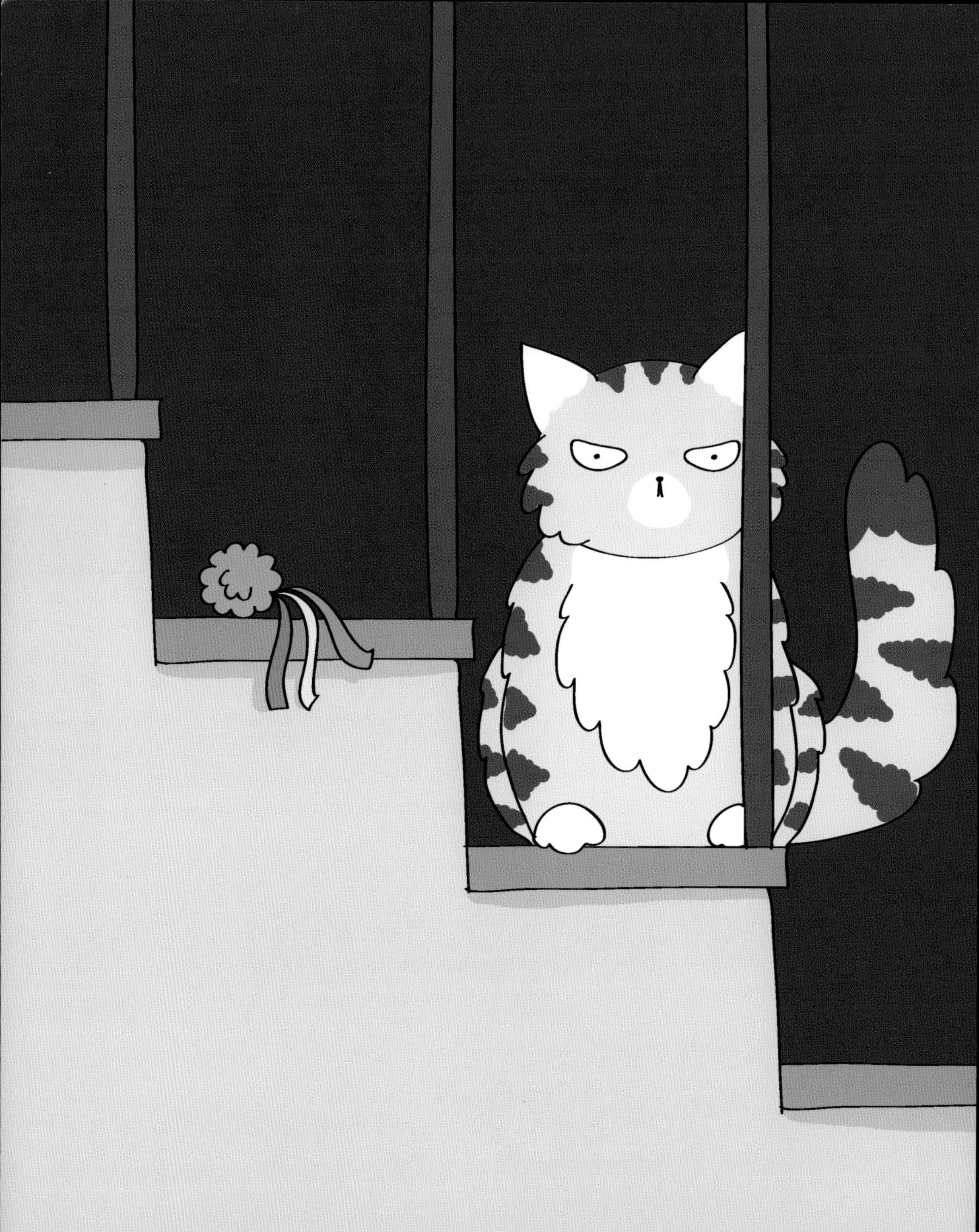

from **Cat**

Lytton Strachey

Dear creature by the fire a-purr,
    Strange idol, eminently bland,
Miraculous puss! As o'er your fur
    I trail a negligible hand,

And gaze into your gazing eyes,
    And wonder in a demi-dream,
What mystery it is that lies,
    Behind those slits that glare and gleam. . . .

With tail erect and pompous march,
    The proudest puss that ever trod,
Through many a grove, 'neath many an arch,
    Impenetrable as a god.

Down many an alabaster flight
    Of broad and cedar-shaded stairs,
While over us the elaborate night
    Mysteriously gleams and glares.

from **To Winky**

Amy Lowell

Cat,
Cat,
What are you?
Son, through a thousand generations, of the black leopards
Padding among the sprigs of young bamboo;
Descendant of many removals from the white panthers
Who crouch by night under the loquat-trees?
You crouch under the orange begonias,
And your eyes are green
With the violence of murder,
Or half-closed and stealthy
Like your sheathed claws.
Slowly, slowly,
You rise and stretch
In a glossiness of beautiful curves,
Of muscles fluctuating under black, glazed hair.

Cat,
You are a strange creature.
You sit on your haunches
And yawn,
But when you leap
I can almost hear the whine
of a released string,
And I look to see its flaccid shaking
In the place whence you sprang.

You carry your tail as a banner,
Slowly it passes my chair,
But when I look for you, you are on the table
Moving easily among the most delicate porcelains.
Your food is a matter of importance
And you are insistent on having
Your wants attended to,
And yet you will eat a bird and its feathers
Apparently without injury.

In the night, I hear you crying,
But if I try to find you
There are only the shadows of rhododendron leaves
Brushing the ground.
When you come in out of the rain,
All wet and with your tail full of burrs,
You fawn on me in coils and subtleties;
But once you are dry
You leave me with a gesture of inconceivable impudence,
Conveyed by the vanishing quirk of your tail
As you slide through the open door.

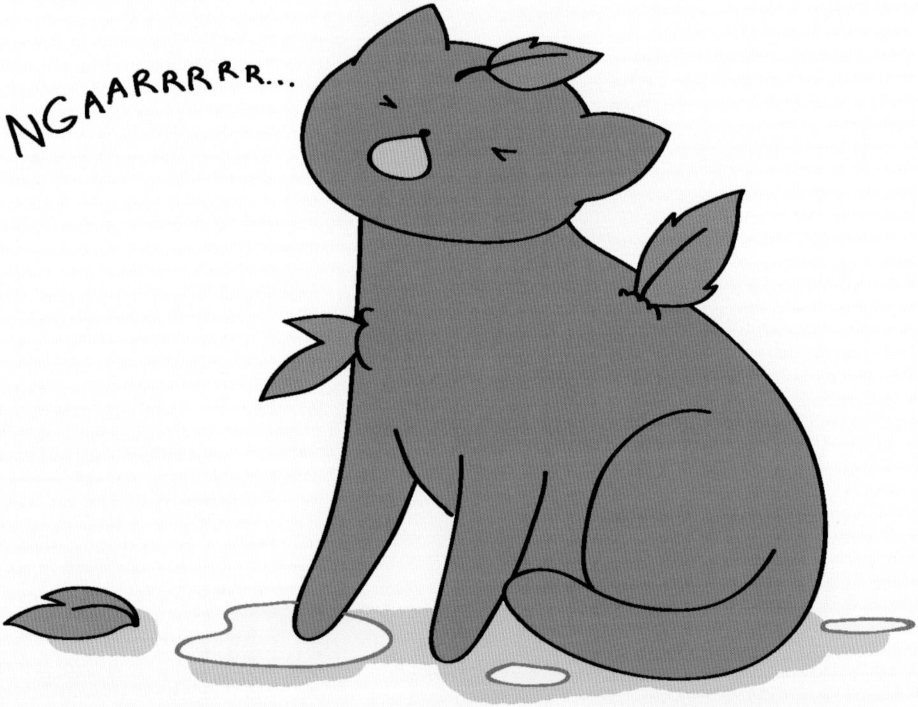
NGAARRRRRR...

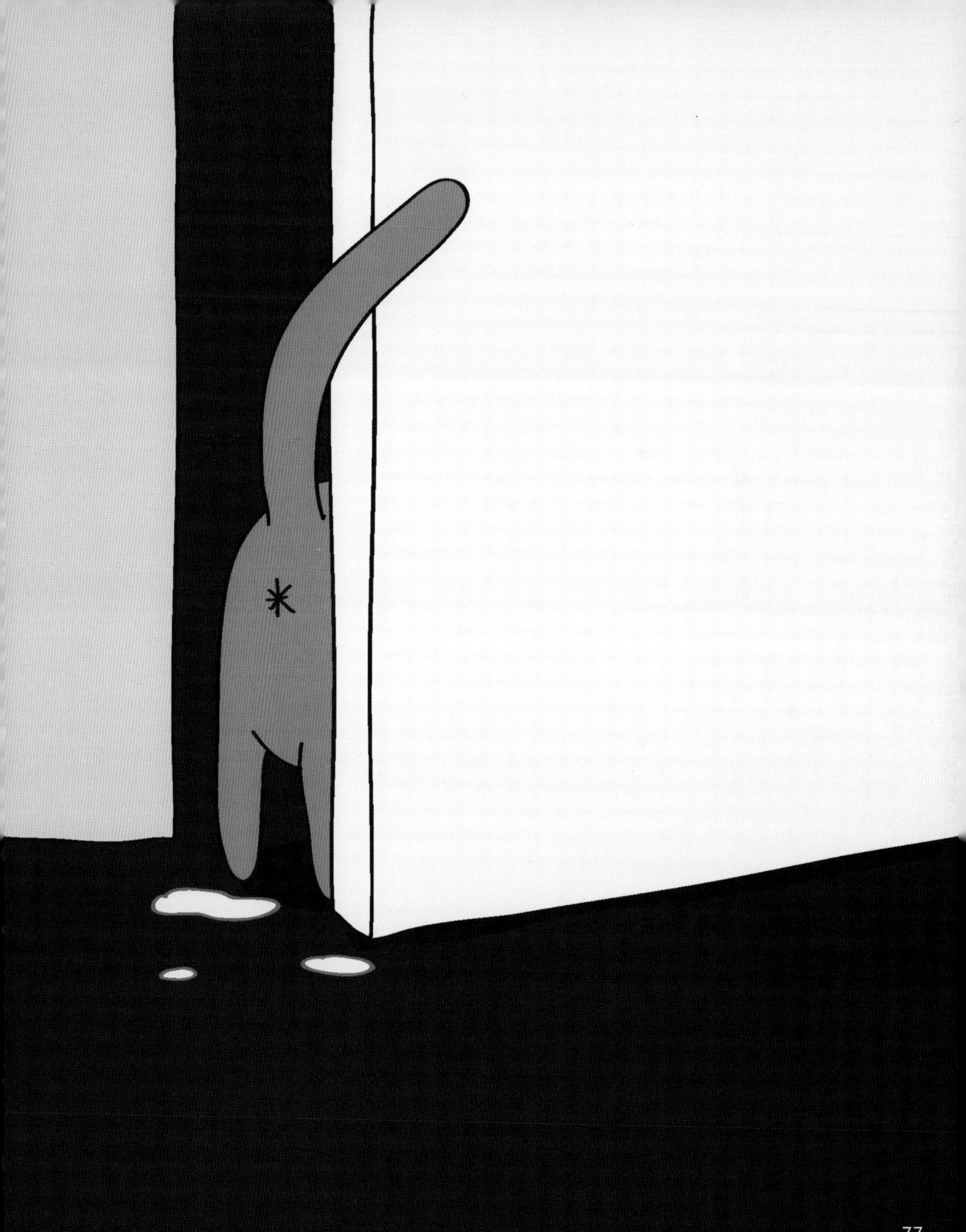

Last Words to a Dumb Friend

Thomas Hardy

Pet was never mourned as you,
Purrer of the spotless hue,
Plumy tail, and wistful gaze
While you humoured our queer ways,
Or outshrilled your morning call
Up the stairs and through the hall—
Foot suspended in its fall—
While, expectant, you would stand
Arched, to meet the stroking hand;
Till your way you chose to wend
Yonder, to your tragic end.

Never another pet for me!
Let your place all vacant be;
Better blankness day by day
Than companion torn away.
Better bid his memory fade,
Better blot each mark he made,
Selfishly escape distress
By contrived forgetfulness,
Than preserve his prints to make
Every morn and eve an ache.

From the chair whereon he sat
Sweep his fur, nor wince thereat;
Rake his little pathways out
Mid the bushes roundabout;
Smooth away his talons' mark
From the claw-worn pine-tree bark,
Where he climbed as dusk embrowned,
Waiting us who loitered round. . . .

Housemate, I can think you still
Bounding to the window-sill,
Over which I vaguely see
Your small mound beneath the tree,
Showing in the autumn shade
That you moulder where you played.

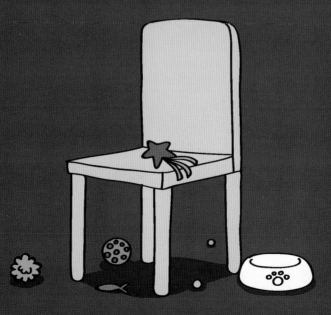

On a Favourite Cat, Drowned in a Tub of Gold Fishes

Thomas Gray

Twas on a lofty vase's side,
Where China's gayest art had dyed
    The azure flowers that blow;
Demurest of the tabby kind,
The pensive Selima reclined,
    Gazed on the lake below.

Her conscious tail her joy declared;
The fair round face, the snowy beard,
    The velvet of her paws,
Her coat, that with the tortoise views,
Her ears of jet, and emerald eyes,
    She saw; and purr'd applause.

Still had she gazed; but 'midst the tide
Two angel forms were seen to glide,
    The Genii of the stream:
Their scaly armour's Tyrian hue
Thro' richest purple to the view
    Betray'd a golden gleam.

The hapless Nymph with wonder saw:
A whisker first and then a claw,
  With many an ardent wish,
She stretch'd in vain to reach the prize.
What female heart can gold despise?
  What Cat's averse to fish?

Presumptuous Maid! with looks intent
Again she stretch'd, again she bent,
  Nor knew the gulf between.
(Malignant Fate sat by, and smiled.)
The slipp'ry verge her feet beguiled,
  She tumbled headlong in.

Eight times emerging from the flood
She mew'd to ev'ry wat'ry god,
  Some speedy aid to send.
No Dolphin came, no Nereid stirr'd;
Nor cruel *Tom,* nor *Susan* heard.
  A Fav'rite has no friend!

From hence, ye Beauties, undeceived,
Know, one false step is ne'er retrieved,
  And be with caution bold.
Not all that tempts your wand'ring eyes
And heedless hearts, is lawful prize;
  Nor all that glisters, gold.

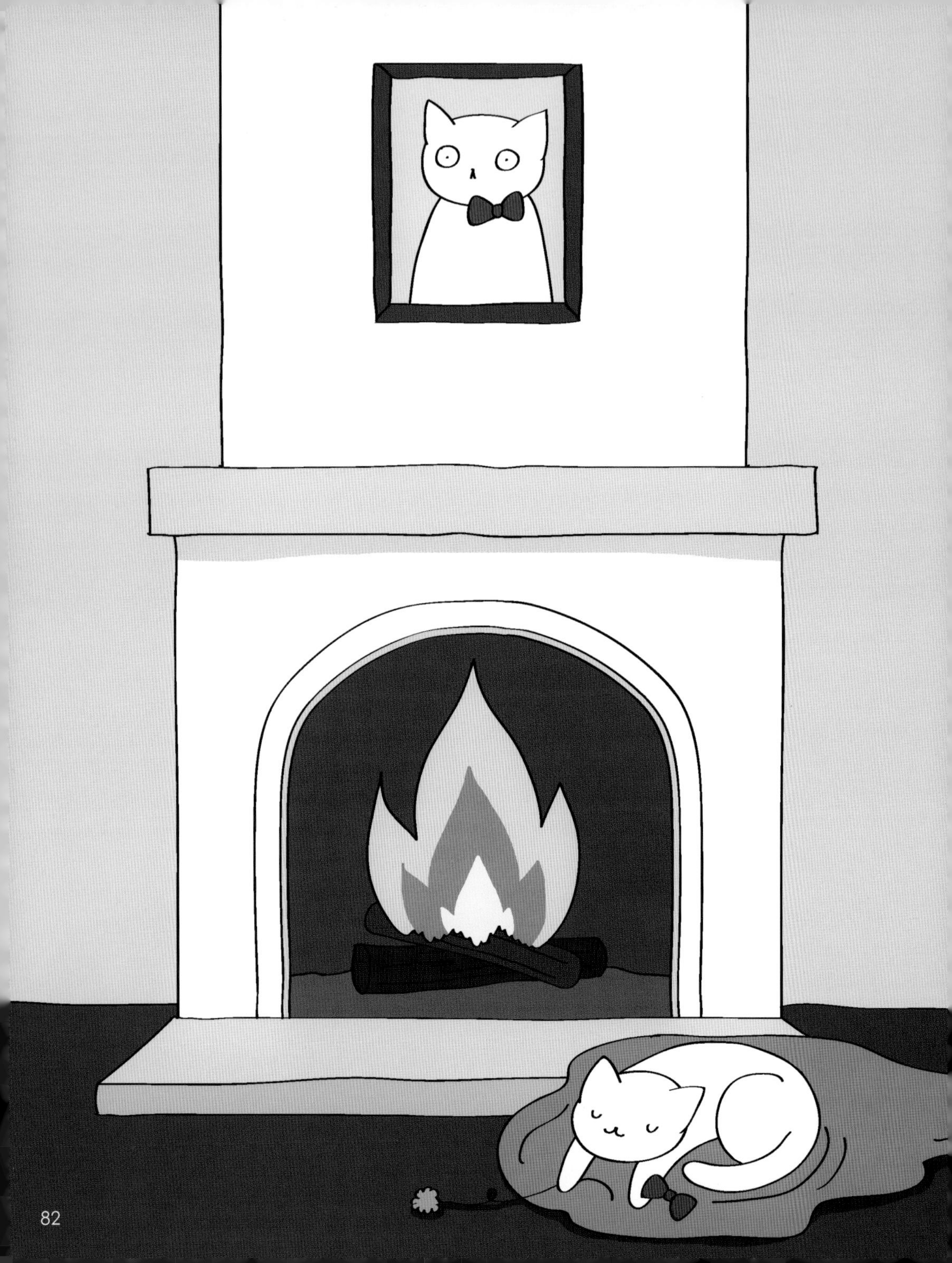

To My Cat

Rosamund Marriott Watson

Half loving-kindliness and half disdain,
Thou comest to my call serenely suave,
With humming speech and gracious gestures grave,
In salutation courtly and urbane;
Yet must I humble me thy grace to gain,
For wiles may win thee though no arts enslave,
And nowhere gladly thou abides save
Where naught disturbs the concord of thy reign.
Sphinx of my quiet hearth! who deign'st to dwell
Friend of my toil, companion of mine ease,
Thine is the lore of Ra and Rameses;
That men forget dost thou remember well,
Beholden still in blinking reveries
With sombre, sea-green gaze inscrutable.

ALSO BY YASMINE SUROVEC:

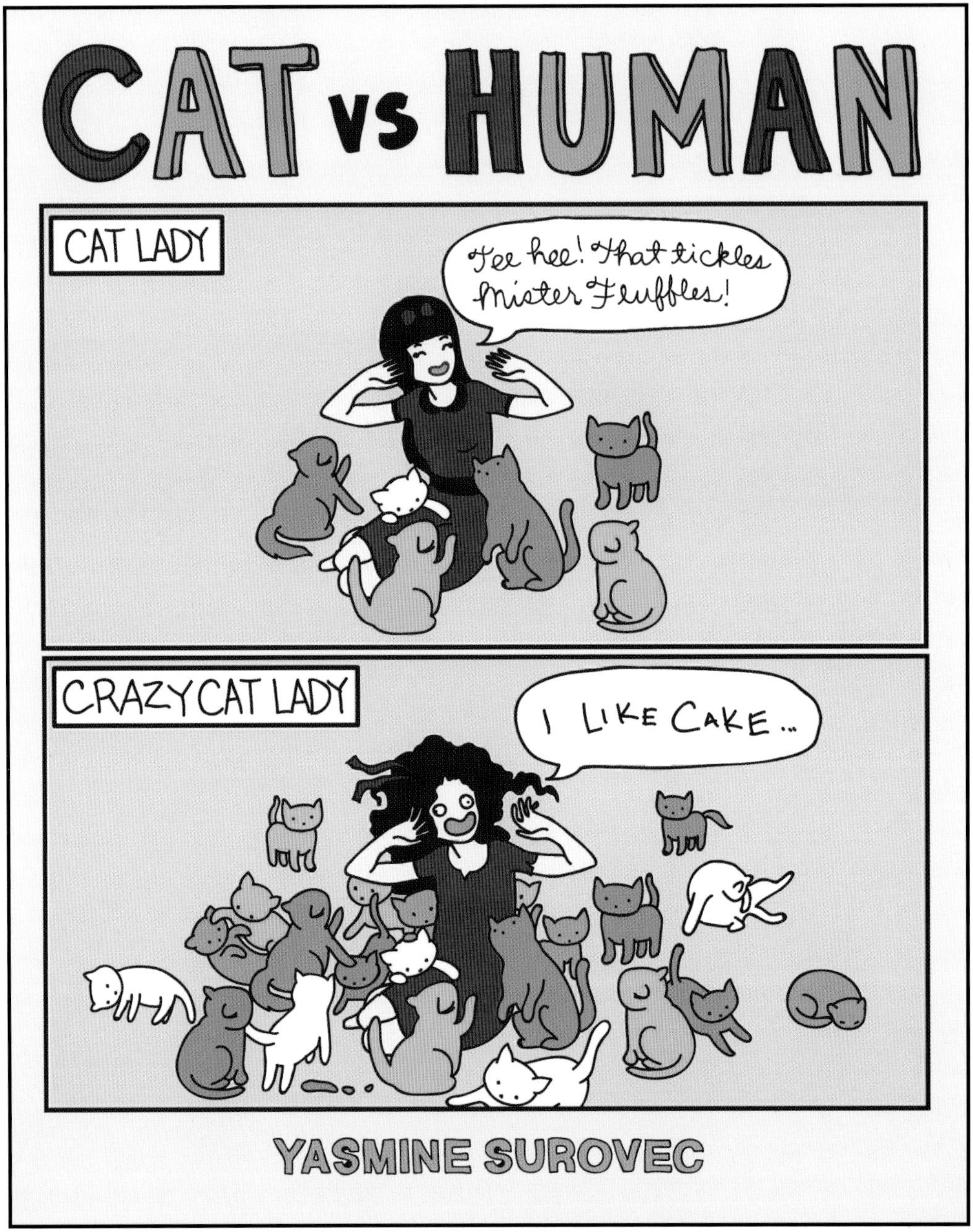
CAT VS HUMAN
CAT LADY
Tee hee! That tickles Mister Fluffles!
CRAZY CAT LADY
I LIKE CAKE...
YASMINE SUROVEC

CAT vs HUMAN

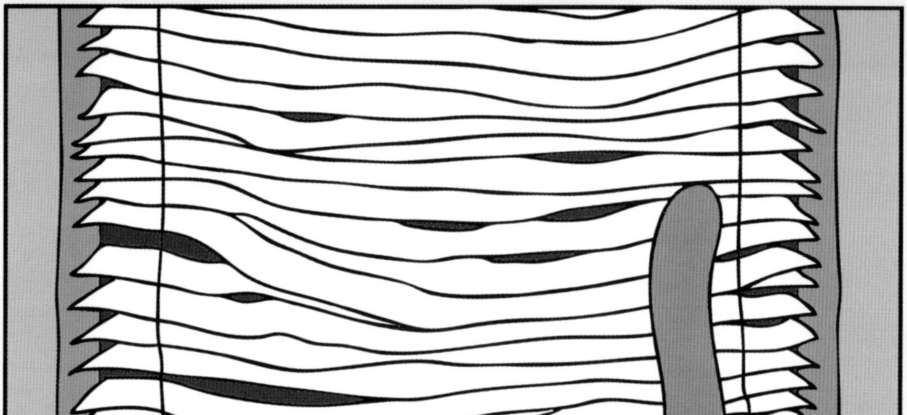

ANOTHER DOSE OF CATNIP

YASMINE SUROVEC

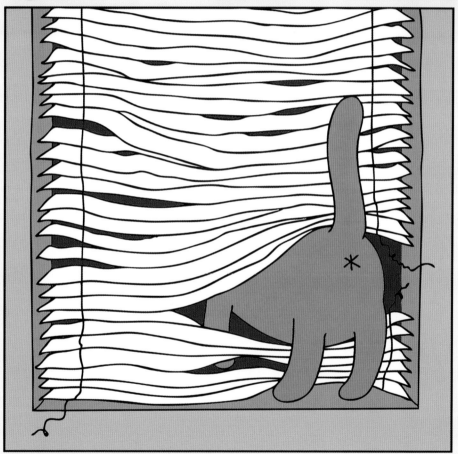

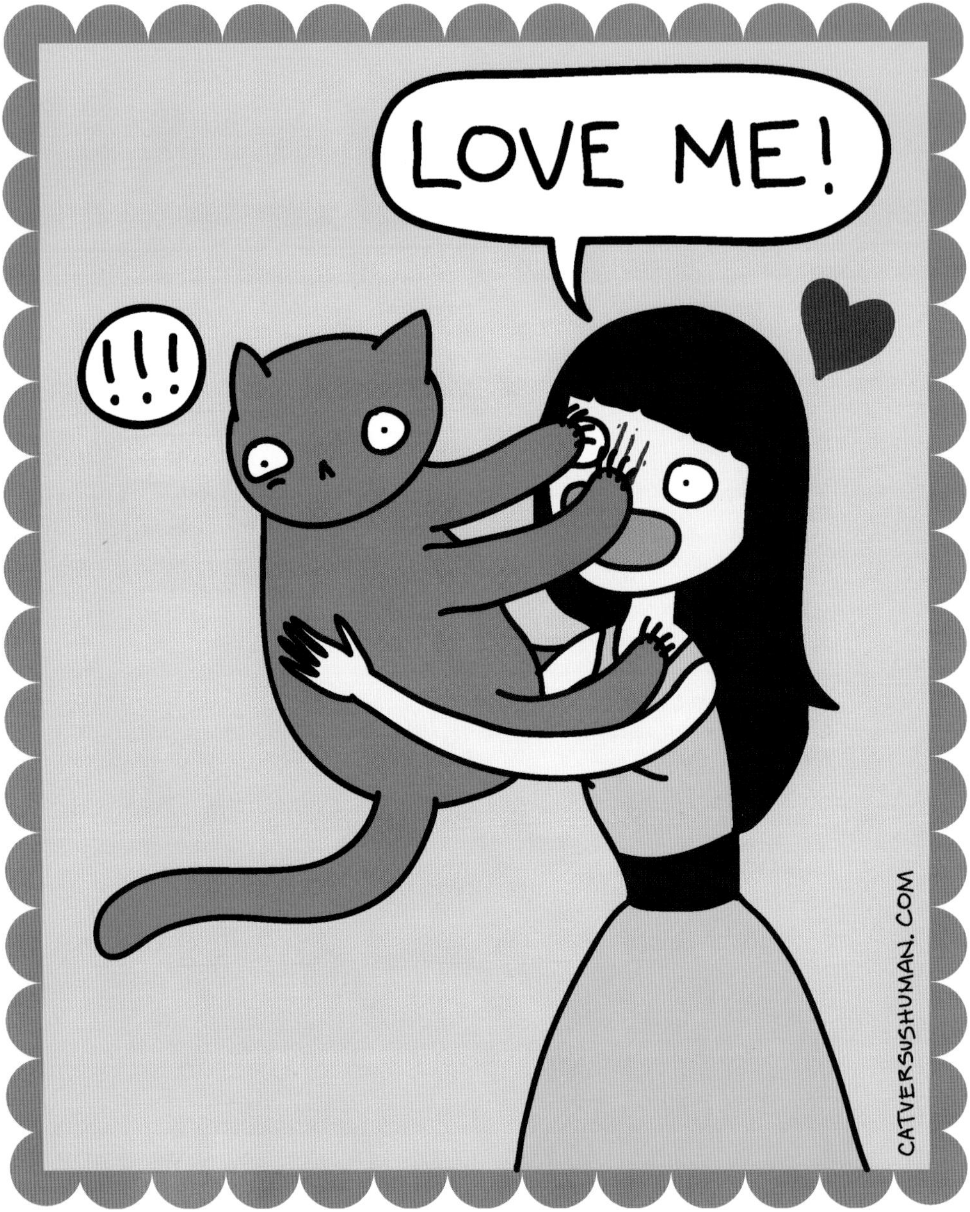
LOVE ME!
!!!
CATVERSUSHUMAN.COM

YASMINE SUROVEC IS
AN ILLUSTRATOR AND
CARTOONIST WHO DIVIDES
HER TIME BETWEEN
CALIFORNIA AND ARIZONA
WITH HER HUSBAND, THREE
KITTIES, AND PUPPY.

Andrews McMeel Publishing, LLC
an Andrews McMeel Universal company
1130 Walnut Street, Kansas City, Missouri 64106

www.andrewsmcmeel.com

15 16 17 18 19 TEN 10 9 8 7 6 5 4 3 2 1

ISBN: 978-1-4494-5793-8

Library of Congress Control Number: 2014954105

ATTENTION: SCHOOLS AND BUSINESSES
Andrews McMeel books are available at quantity discounts with bulk purchase for educational, business, or sales promotional use. For information, please e-mail the Andrews McMeel Publishing Special Sales Department: specialsales@amuniversal.com.